CRAIG GROESCHEL

WINNING THE WAR

IN YOUR MIND

WORKBOOK | 12 SESSIONS

CHANGE YOUR THINKING, CHANGE YOUR LIFE

ZONDERVAN®
.com

Winning the War for Your Mind Workbook
© 2021 by Craig Groeschel

Requests for information should be addressed to:
Zondervan, 3900 Sparks Dr. SE, Grand Rapids, Michigan 49546

ISBN 978-0-310-13682-8 (softcover)
ISBN 978-0-310-13683-5 (ebook)

Published in association with Winters & King, Inc.

CONTENTS

INTRODUCTION

The life you have is a reflection of what you think.

Like whitewater rapids rushing you downstream, your thoughts move your life in the direction of their strongest currents. The thoughts you believe, hold onto, and use to support your decisions determine your view of everything and everyone around you, including yourself. You probably don't stop and think about the power your thoughts have over your life—which only increases the power they have to determine your decisions and shape your actions.

Simply put, what you think determines what you believe. Every thought in your brain produces a neurochemical change in your mind. And these thoughts shape your life. Once your thoughts determine what you believe, these beliefs then determine how you behave. In many ways, you become what you think about. Therefore, the better you grasp the importance of your thoughts, the better equipped you'll be to change your life in powerful ways.

Even as scientists and neurologists continue to confirm the power our thoughts have on us, God told us this truth more than 1,500 years ago: "For as [a person] thinks in his heart, so he is" (Proverbs 23:7 NKJV). God knows that what we focus on mentally affects every aspect of our lives because he created us that way.

Drawing on what the Bible tells us about the power of our thoughts as well as what we can learn from modern psychology, particularly an area called cognitive behavioral therapy, we have the ability to change our lives for the better. We can live according to the principles and promises God gives us and enjoy being all that he created us to be. Otherwise, our thoughts will continue to sweep us away in dangerous currents of deception, misinformation, and lies from our enemy, the devil.

If you are sick and tired of being sick and tired, of having your life poisoned by toxic thoughts, of being held hostage by those inner voices, then trust God that you can change. As you read *Winning the War in Your Mind*, this workbook will help you understand and apply the important truths essential to changing your thoughts and behavior.

Following the chapters of the book, you will be equipped and empowered with tools to help you identify the lies holding you back and replace those lies with the truth that will set you free. First, you will understand the battle for your mind and why it's the reason you might not be who you think you are. Next, you will discover the spiritual weapons God has given you to win the battles you face and fight daily. From there you will learn how your brain works and the incredible ability you have to reframe your thinking and literally redesign your mind around new thoughts. Finally, you will be equipped to identify your mental triggers and overcome them through the power of prayer.

You will discover how to live free of anxiety and negativity and to experience the joy and peace that comes from knowing God and living in his truth. With his help, you can master your mind, think his thoughts, and do his will. You can renew the intricately designed brain he has created as part of your body. You can stop believing the lies that hold you back, weigh you down, and keep you living a life that leaves you frustrated and unfulfilled.

As you dwell in his truth, you can grow to live by faith and not be overcome with worry. You can allow God's truth to help treat your anxious mind. Instead of wavering aimlessly, you can learn to become more confidently decisive. You can grow beyond all that weighs you down and dwell in daily peace. With God's help, you will experience life to the fullest, living out the purpose for which you were created. It's time to arrest your false thoughts and liberate God's truth in you.

It's time to change your thinking so God can change your life.

PART 1

THE REPLACEMENT PRINCIPLE

REMOVE THE LIES, REPLACE WITH TRUTH

When you understand the battle taking place in your mind, you realize that you're not who you think you are. In fact, your thoughts may be based on false beliefs and inaccurate assumptions, which then prevent you from living in the truth of who God says you are. When you explore how to identify and remove the lies, you can then focus on the truth of God's Word.

As you practice the Replacement Principle, you will:

- Realize how your perception shapes your reality and therefore the decisions you make and actions you take.
- Perform a thought audit to help you quickly evaluate the different kinds of thoughts occupying your mind and fueling your emotions.
- Become a thought warrior who can push back against thoughts that are untrue, outdated, and destructive.
- Identify the lies you believe and see the harmful impact they have on how you see God, yourself, your life, and your relationships with others.
- Release old lies and redirect your focus to the new truth of God's Word.
- Declare truth in all areas of your thinking as you trust God and live according to his promises.

PERCEPTION IS REALITY

You cannot change what you do not confront.
If you ignore the battle, you lose the battle.

CRAIG GROESCHEL

Every day you are engaged in a battle. You may not recognize the battle, but it is wreaking havoc in your life. Ever wonder why you can't shake a habit? Why you feel you can't connect with God? Why you lose your temper so easily? Why you continually make bad decisions? Why your kids or friends appear to have a cloud of darkness over them when you're around? Why you and your spouse fight so much? Why you're consumed with worry, fear, and negativity?

There is a reason why. Your mind is a warzone, and it's critical that you recognize the battle is raging. If you ignore what's going on in your thought life, then your unhealthy thoughts will continue to erode your quality of life, your relationships, your faith. Because the assault will not stop unless you engage.

The apostle Paul made it clear, "Our struggle is not against flesh and blood, but against the rulers, against the authorities, against the powers of this dark world and against the spiritual forces of evil in the heavenly realms" (Ephesians 6:12). You are in a battle, and your adversary is not your boss, spouse, kid, or neighbor with the annoying dog that's always barking. The one you are fighting against is your spiritual enemy—the devil.

Satan is your unseen enemy whose mission is to destroy you (see John 10:10), stop you (see 1 Thessalonians 2:18), and devour you (see 1 Peter 5:8). Satan despises you with more hatred than you can imagine. He wants to keep you from intimate relationships with those you love most. He wants to rob you of deep joy, inner contentment, and abiding peace. The devil wants to strip you from the fulfilment of knowing that what you do makes a difference.

He accomplishes this by convincing you of his lies. He is a deceiver, and his strategy to defeat you is to persuade you to believe lies. We are warned, "there is no truth in him . . . when he lies, he speaks his native language, for he is a liar and the father of lies" (John 8:44). If he can get you to accept his false notions and dangerous deceits, then his lies manipulate your perception of reality. You accept the way you see things—based on your enemy's subterfuge—and live your life based on untrue beliefs.

Winning the war in your mind requires you to study how you see things and why you see them that way, identify the lies of the enemy, and rely instead on the truth of God.

EXPLORING GOD'S WORD

Perhaps no one in the Bible understood how one's view of reality can be shaped by perceptions better than the apostle Paul. After all, he started life as a devout Jew, zealously committed to maintaining the letter of religious law and persecuting those who were following the life and teachings of Jesus Christ. Known then as Saul, he experienced a supernatural encounter with the Lord while traveling to Damascus in the hopes of catching some believers there. As you read through the following account, underline or circle any words, details, or images that relate to how Paul's perception of Jesus and understanding of faith changed.

¹ Meanwhile, Saul was still breathing out murderous threats against the Lord's disciples. He went to the high priest ² and asked him for letters to the synagogues in Damascus, so that if he found any there who belonged to the Way, whether men or women, he might take them as prisoners to Jerusalem. ³ As he neared Damascus on his journey, suddenly a light from heaven flashed around him. ⁴ He fell to the ground and heard a voice say to him, "Saul, Saul, why do you persecute me?"

⁵ "Who are you, Lord?" Saul asked.

"I am Jesus, whom you are persecuting," he replied. ⁶ "Now get up and go into the city, and you will be told what you must do."

⁷ The men traveling with Saul stood there speechless; they heard the sound but did not see anyone. ⁸ Saul got up from the ground, but when he opened his eyes he could see nothing. So they led him by the hand into Damascus. ⁹ For three days he was blind, and did not eat or drink anything.

¹⁰ In Damascus there was a disciple named Ananias. The Lord called to him in a vision, "Ananias!"

"Yes, Lord," he answered.

¹¹ The Lord told him, "Go to the house of Judas on Straight Street and ask for a man from Tarsus named Saul, for he is praying. ¹² In a vision he has seen a man named Ananias come and place his hands on him to restore his sight."

¹³ "Lord," Ananias answered, "I have heard many reports about this man and all the harm he has done to your holy people in Jerusalem. ¹⁴ And he has come here with authority from the chief priests to arrest all who call on your name."

¹⁵ But the Lord said to Ananias, "Go! This man is my chosen instrument to proclaim my name to the Gentiles and their kings and to the people of Israel. ¹⁶ I will show him how much he must suffer for my name."

¹⁷ Then Ananias went to the house and entered it. Placing his hands on Saul, he said, "Brother Saul, the Lord—Jesus, who appeared to you on the road as you were coming here—has sent me so that you may see again and be filled with the Holy Spirit." ¹⁸ Immediately, something like scales fell from Saul's eyes, and he could see again. He got up and was baptized, ¹⁹ and after taking some food, he regained his strength.

– ACTS 9:1–19

- What did Saul believe that caused him to go around "breathing murderous threats against the Lord's disciples" (Acts 9:1)? What was the basis for these beliefs?

- Considering how deeply embedded Saul's thoughts about Jesus must have been, why did this encounter change his thinking? Based solely on a rational, logical extension of Saul's false beliefs, what other kind of response might he have had to this situation?

- How did the truth of Saul's own encounter with Christ force him to reconsider his perception of reality? Why?

- Saul's transformational encounter is also striking because of the faith of Ananias. Logically, based on the reports he had heard about Saul's relentless quest to arrest and kill followers of Jesus, Ananias was understandably wary. What changed Ananias' mind about the task God asked him to perform? What did Ananias' experience have in common with Saul's?

- This incident reminds us of how vision often serves as a metaphor for seeing clearly beyond concrete perceptions. How did Saul's blindness force him to reconsider what he used to believe? What did he learn about his ability to see clearly after he welcomed the Holy Spirit into his life?

● How did Saul's way of thinking change after he surrendered to Christ and was filled with God's Spirit? Why did his previous beliefs no longer hold the same power over him?

REFLECTING ON THE TRUTH

After this dramatic encounter, Saul went on to fulfill the prophecy that God related to Ananias: "This man is my chosen instrument to proclaim my name to the Gentiles and their kings and to the people of Israel" (Acts 19:15). He adopted his Roman name *Paul* as he began to travel further into the Gentile world. He spent the rest of his days traveling, preaching, and evangelizing despite experiencing the same kind of persecution he once enforced. He also endured trials and hardships—including arrests, beatings, shipwrecks, snakebites, jail time, and earthquakes—that never shook his faith but only strengthened his trust in God.

Clearly, Paul's thinking changed in radical ways as he experienced the supernatural power of God and recognized the spiritual warfare in which he was engaged. Paul made this clear when he wrote, "We are not fighting against flesh-and-blood enemies, but against evil rulers and authorities of the unseen world, against mighty powers in this dark world, and against evil spirits in the heavenly places" (Ephesians 6:12 NLT).

Yet while Paul provided us with considerable insights into how to win this battle, which we will explore throughout this workbook, he frequently reminded us to focus on the power our thoughts have in defeating the enemy and overcoming temptations. Writing to the community of believers at Philippi, he urged, "Finally, brothers and sisters, whatever is true, whatever is noble, whatever is right, whatever is pure, whatever is lovely, whatever is admirable—if anything is excellent or praiseworthy—think about such things. Whatever you have learned or received or heard from me, or seen in me—put it into practice. And the God of peace will be with you" (Philippians 4:8–9).

- What's your reaction when you read Paul's warning about the spiritual battle we are all fighting? What beliefs and supporting thoughts shape how you view the dark forces you are up against?

- Fill in the blanks:

  When I think about devils and demons as Paul describes here, I immediately recall

  _____ .

  If someone asked me to describe my view of the devil, I would tell that person

  _____ .

  Spiritual warfare, in my opinion and based on my experience, can be defined as

  _____ .

- What concerns you most when you think about the devil opposing you and trying to convince you of his lies? What frightens you or causes alarm? Why?

- What is one of the enemy's lies that you've already identified in your thinking? How did you come to think this?

- With Paul's warning in mind, why do you suppose he also urges us to curate our thoughts and focus only on the positive attributes listed? What's the relationship between the two?

• In response to Paul's call for positive thinking, list the first thing that pops into your mind from your personal experience that illustrates each of his categories:

Noble: _____.

Right: _____.

Pure: _____.

Lovely: _____.

Admirable: _____.

Excellent: _____

Praiseworthy: _____.

CHANGING YOUR STRATEGY

Most of us have bad habits and destructive behaviors that we want to change in various areas of our lives. We know that they are not good for us and that they pull us away from God. It might be how we handle our anger or our tendency to gossip about people at work. We might struggle with looking at sites online that we know do not reflect what God wants for our lives. It could be the way we handle money and remain stuck in debt or how we've resigned ourselves to remaining in unhealthy relationships.

Whether it's focusing on a healthy diet, or coming to terms with a secret addiction, or keeping control over our words, our likelihood for success will increase when we examine our thoughts, beliefs, feelings, and motives around each habit or behavior. Repetition certainly plays a key part in developing a conditioned pattern, but the thoughts and beliefs beneath our actions are often what prevent us from making lasting changes.

As you begin to challenge the way you perceive reality, you may want to begin with the things you are doing that bug you the most and negatively impact your relationship with God. So, for each area of your life below, list something you would like to change and then funnel down to the feelings, thoughts, and beliefs contributing to your behavior.

SELF-IMAGE AND SELF-CONFIDENCE

Behavior you want to change:

Feelings associated with this behavior:

Thoughts connected to this behavior:

False beliefs supporting these thoughts:

PRIMARY RELATIONSHIPS WITH FAMILY AND CLOSE FRIENDS

Behavior you want to change:

Feelings associated with this behavior:

Thoughts connected to this behavior:

False beliefs supporting these thoughts:

PHYSICAL HEALTH AND LIFESTYLE HABITS (DIET, EXERCISE, SLEEP)

Behavior you want to change:

Feelings associated with this behavior:

Thoughts connected to this behavior:

False beliefs supporting these thoughts:

WORK, CAREER, EDUCATION, AND TRAINING

Behavior you want to change:

Feelings associated with this behavior:

Thoughts connected to this behavior:

False beliefs supporting these thoughts:

WAYS YOU PRACTICE AND EXERCISE YOUR FAITH IN GOD

Behavior you want to change:

Feelings associated with this behavior:

Thoughts connected to this behavior:

False beliefs supporting these thoughts:

EXERCISING THE EXCHANGE

The key to winning the war in our mind comes down to identifying the harmful thoughts, connecting them to the false beliefs and lies of the enemy we've accepted, and replacing them with the truth of God's Word. Too often, we allow our thoughts to run like wild horses back and forth in our minds. We draw conclusions, create expectations, and assume worst-case consequences without stopping to check and verify the basis for these runaway mustangs. We know that comparing ourselves to others often makes us feel depressed, envious, and inadequate, but rarely do we challenge ourselves to examine and top the comparisons.

As you begin identifying, eliminating, and replacing negative thoughts and false beliefs, you will find that it helps to prepare ways you can respond when you catch yourself thinking destructive thoughts that are not true. Gradually, you will learn to be more aware of what you're thinking and how these thoughts directly relate to your moods, attitudes, perceptions, decisions, and actions (or lack of actions). The best place to begin is by becoming a collector of your thoughts and a student of each one's origin and impact.

Toward that goal, you will find a helpful exercise at the end of chapter 1 in *Winning the War in Your Mind*. If you haven't already completed "Your Thought Audit" at the end of that chapter, go back and spend some unhurried time answering the questions about your thought patterns. Once you've completed "Your Thought Audit," look for patterns, triggers, and consequences that various thoughts have in your life on a daily basis. Use the following questions to help you become more aware of your typical thoughts and the ways they shape your life, both in big ways and in small ways.

- What consistent patterns and repeated thoughts emerged from your audit? How aware were you of these patterns and repetitions before the audit?

- What surprised you most from the findings in your thought audit? Why did this surprise you?

- Overall, do your thought patterns reflect your beliefs about God and the faith you have in Jesus? How would you describe this gap?

- What one single thought that you recorded during your audit reflects a recurrent theme or larger struggle throughout your life? What's the belief underlying this thought?

After answering these questions and reviewing your audit, spend some time in honest prayer before the Lord. Ask him to work through your efforts to help you win the spiritual battle in your mind once and for all. Pray for wisdom and discernment as you seek to identify the negative, destructive ways of thinking that continue to pull you down. Thank God for all that he's doing in your life and the victory you have because of what Jesus did on the cross.

BECOMING A
THOUGHT WARRIOR

To win the battle for our minds, we must engage,
because there is no other way for us to defeat evil.

CRAIG GROESCHEL

Like most people, you probably carry around baggage from your past that continues to shape the way you think. Experiences from your childhood linger just below the surface, and parental voices become embedded in your consciousness, echoing messages that may have been true then but not now. You have memories and associations of those events, messages, feelings and more as you progressed into adulthood, forming conclusions and expectations based on all these assumptions.

But many of them, perhaps *most* of them, are simply not true.

You are not who others say you are. You are not what your dad said. You are not who you mom told you to be. You are not what your teacher said. You are not what your grandmother said. You are not what the bully online said.

You must also realize this: You are not who *you* say you are. You are not what your insecurities echo across your lifetime. You are not what the accusing whispers say you are. You are not the failure your past mistakes claim you are. You are not the lies you believe.

Satan's strategy to win the battle for your mind is convincing you to believe lies. If you believe a lie, it could hold you back from serving where you believe you could make a difference. It will keep you living in shame from the past when God wants you free for a better future. The lies will poison you to believe you can never be full of joy, when God desires to bless you in more ways than you can even imagine.

Those voices have probably haunted you, demeaned you, stripped you of your confidence, stunted your spiritual growth, cast a shadow over what should be joyful moments in your life, paralyzed your ability to make healthy decisions, and inhibited your ability to enjoy God, people, life.

Those thoughts can destroy you, but those thoughts *lie*.

You are *not* who you think you are.

There is hope. Your future doesn't have to look like your past. You can change.

If you're willing to fight.

But you have to make a choice to recognize the battle you're in and engage with this spiritual reality if you want to change your thoughts, improve your life, and grow closer to God. Simply put, you have to fight. You may not consider yourself a fighter or someone who enjoys going to battle, but you're being assaulted by your spiritual enemy, the devil, each day. You may be oblivious to his attacks or fail to recognize his involvement, but he's out to get you.

If this sounds overly dramatic, alarmist, or exaggerated, then you're thinking exactly what the enemy wants you to think. It's probably easier for you to recognize that your life is not what you want, that you've settled for less than God's best for your life, and that constant busyness keeps you distracted and pulled in a million directions. You may be pretending you're okay, even happy, but you know that you long for more—more peace, more purpose, more passion, more hope, more life.

As long as you ignore what's going on in your thought life, then your unhealthy thoughts will continue to erode your quality of life, your relationships, your faith. Because the assault will not stop unless you engage. To win the battle for your mind, you must become a thought warrior, because there is no other way to defeat evil.

EXPLORING GOD'S WORD

Even when you're willing to fight, it can be tough to move forward because you quickly realize that you don't have what it takes to win the war. Like most people, you've tried to change your thinking, tried to break old habits, tried to change your life. You've done everything you know to do, but you always end up back in the same place. You keep doing what you don't want to do and not doing what you want to do. You keep falling down and falling short. Sometimes you might feel like giving up.

Because here's the problem: The power you need to win the battle in your mind is a power you don't possess. Relying on your own power is just self-help, and self-help only goes so far against the power of the enemy. But no matter what your circumstances may be or how hopeless you feel, don't lose your faith. You are not alone in your frustration. Because even the apostle Paul struggled with feeling stuck. Here's how he describes himself:

> [15] *I do not understand what I do. For what I want to do I do not do, but what I hate I do.* [16] *And if I do what I do not want to do, I agree that the law is good.* [17] *As it is, it is no longer I myself who do it, but it is sin living in me.* [18] *For I know that good itself does not dwell in me, that is, in my sinful nature. For I have the desire to do what is good, but I cannot carry it out.* [19] *For I do not do the good I want to do, but the evil I do not want to do—this I keep on doing.* [20] *Now if I do what I do not want to do, it is no longer I who do it, but it is sin living in me that does it.*
>
> [21] *So I find this law at work: Although I want to do good, evil is right there with me.* [22] *For in my inner being I delight in God's law;* [23] *but I see another law at work in me, waging war against the law of my mind and making me a prisoner of the law of sin at work within me.* [24] *What a wretched man I am! Who will rescue me from this body that is subject to death?*
>
> — ROMANS 7:15–24

- How does Paul describe his response to the opposing forces at work in his life? What thoughts does he identify related to each of these opposite forces?

- How does Paul's description of this cycle lead him to a frustrating conclusion? Why does he call himself a "wretched man" by the end of his internal analysis?

- According to Paul, why does he keep on sinning even when he knows he's disobeying God, which is not what he wants to do?

- Why does Paul not give up and just resign himself to sinning and thinking of himself as spiritually defeated? What sustains him?

- Make a list of the laws that Paul mentions in this description. Why does he feel like he's a prisoner to one and unable to fully embrace the other?

● What assumptions does Paul make here about the "law of sin" at work in him? And what motivates him to try and resist temptation and avoid sin?

REFLECTING ON THE TRUTH

If Paul never learned to rely on God's power to win his spiritual battle, then he might not have much to teach us. He hardly sounds like a successful thought warrior in Romans 7:15–24. Fortunately, for himself and for us, Paul experienced incredible victory in this battle and therefore has a lot to teach us. Just consider how he describes himself in Philippians 4:12: "I have learned the secret of being content in any and every situation." Now that sounds like a guy who has mastered his thoughts and won the battle in his mind!

What's Paul's secret? It's one that he summarizes as well as describes in more detail throughout his writings. So first consider the big picture he provides in revealing his secret to success in this spiritual battle: "For though we live in the world, we do not wage war as the world does. The weapons we fight with are not the weapons of the world. On the contrary, they have divine power to demolish strongholds. We demolish arguments and every pretension that sets itself up against the knowledge of God, and we take captive every thought to make it obedient to Christ" (2 Corinthians 10:3–5).

This shift in Paul's perspective should encourage you if you feel like your thoughts seem to run out of control some days. In order to move from this mental tug-of-war to the peaceful, purposeful focus Paul eventually experienced, notice three things in his explanation from this passage: (1) while we're in this world, we don't fight like the world fights; (2) therefore, the weapons we use are not the world's weapons; and (3) our weapons have divine power.

This last point is huge because you not only have divine power but also the spiritual force required to "demolish strongholds." Here, the word *demolish* is translated from the Greek word *kathaireo*, which means destruction requiring massive power. No matter how strong you are or what kind of arsenal you might have amassed, your power cannot compare to what Paul's describing here.

Only God has this kind of supernatural power, and he has made it available to you. Paul explains, "I also pray that you will understand the incredible greatness of God's power for us who believe him. This is the same mighty power that raised Christ from the dead" (Ephesians 1:19–20 NLT). Stop and think about that for a moment: *The same power that raised Jesus from the dead is available to you.*

- What thoughts came to mind when you read Paul's description of his mental battle in Romans 7:15–24? How did you feel as you considered his explanation of these opposing forces at war inside him?

- Then what did you think when you read Paul's description of the spiritual power you have available? What feelings stir inside when you imagine the kind of divine power Paul's talking about here?

- What are the mental strongholds you face on a regular basis? What patterns of thoughts cause you to do things you don't want to do and pull you away from God?

- What would it look like in your life to have these mental strongholds demolished? Who would you be without your battle with these negative, destructive thoughts?

- How do you feel about the spiritual battle you face knowing that the *same power that raised Jesus from the dead is available to you?*

- Knowing you cannot rely on your own power to win the battle in your mind, what's required for you to access this *kathaireo,* resurrection power?

CHANGING YOUR STRATEGY

Paul said you have access to God's divine power to "demolish strongholds" (2 Corinthians 10:4). *Stronghold* is translated from the Greek word *ochuróma*, which literally means "to fortify." In ancient times this kind of secure stronghold was the fortress built on top of the highest peak in the city. Twenty-foot walls often surrounded this citadel where its leaders met, where treasure was stored, and where precious documents and holy relics were guarded. From this highest vantage point, soldiers could spot approaching enemies before they attacked, ensuring their ability to defend and protect the city's greatest assets.

Paul made the comparison between those fortresses and the lies we believe. Like the walls of the strongholds, these lies we believe have been reinforced again and again. We have believed the lies so long that it's as though they have become a part of us. We keep them protected. They are almost impenetrable.

This is why you may have struggled and failed to experience lasting changes in your life. You feel caught between the push-and-pull of your sinful desires and your sincere commitment to love and obey God. You try to change, and maybe succeed temporarily, but eventually slide back into the same thought ruts and behavioral habits. Maybe you made some form of a resolution or you vowed that you would start doing something or stop doing something. You committed to lose weight, or, on the positive side, to pray daily or save more money.

Unfortunately, if you want to change your life, you cannot just change your behavior. If only it were that simple! You may be able to change your behavior for a little while, but the behavior eventually resurfaces.

Why? You didn't get to the root of the problem: the lies you believe. If you are going to change your life you *have to* change your thinking.

As you continue identifying your thought patterns based on false assumptions, invalid conclusions, and the lies of the enemy, it may be helpful to recognize why your past efforts failed. Use the following questions to help you shift your strategy from one based on your own power to one based on God's supernatural power.

- When was the last time you tried to make a major change in the way you live your life? What were the circumstances related to your desire to make this change?

- Was your decision to try to make this major change fueled by a particular event, experience, or relationship? What specifically motivated you to try to make this change?

- What baggage did you carry with you as you tried to make this major change? Had you tried to make this change before or ones that were similar?

Be objective as you look back on your failed efforts to make this major change so you can identify why it didn't work or last very long. Consider what you were thinking and feeling at that time and identify the kinds of destructive mental strongholds you were up against. Use the template below to aid in your identification and understanding. All of these categories may not apply, but keep in mind the way the swift current of your thoughts often washes over all areas of your thinking.

SELF-IMAGE AND SELF-CONFIDENCE

Mental strongholds:

Emotional strongholds:

Spiritual strongholds:

PRIMARY RELATIONSHIPS WITH FAMILY AND CLOSE FRIENDS

Mental strongholds:

Emotional strongholds:

Spiritual strongholds:

PHYSICAL HEALTH AND LIFESTYLE HABITS (DIET, EXERCISE, SLEEP, ETC.)

Mental strongholds:

Emotional strongholds:

Spiritual strongholds:

WORK, CAREER, EDUCATION, AND TRAINING

Mental strongholds:

Emotional strongholds:

Spiritual strongholds:

YOUR RELATIONSHIP WITH GOD

Mental strongholds:

Emotional strongholds:

Spiritual strongholds:

EXERCISING THE EXCHANGE

Changing the way you think about your tactics for winning the war in your mind is not easy and rarely happens overnight. Exchanging old lies for God's truth takes time. Lasting change requires ongoing awareness and committed practice. You cannot defeat what you cannot define. You must identify the lie that has a strong hold on you and consider how it spreads like a cancer into virtually all areas of your life.

As we read in Proverbs 21:22, "One who is wise can go up against the city of the mighty and pull down the stronghold in which they trust." Notice the two-step strategy here: attack the city and pull down its stronghold. Otherwise, if you attack the city but don't take the more difficult action of bringing down the stronghold, the city will reestablish itself. Like weeds yanked without pulling their roots, those city leaders hiding in the stronghold would find ways to retaliate.

You have to bring down the stronghold, and the way you begin is by identifying each and every lie that fortifies its power in your thinking. This process won't be easy, although some lies will be more recognizable than others. If you've already started this process by completing the exercise "Identifying the Lies You Believe" at the end of chapter 2, then use these questions to take apart the lies you've been living with and the ways they have created strongholds in your life. Think of it like pulling threads to unravel the blanket that's smothering your mind.

If you haven't listed the lies you believe, then spend some focused and undistracted time identifying the ones most ingrained in your thinking. Review the "Identifying the Lies You Believe" exercise in chapter 2 of the book. After you've identified as many lies as possible, then you're ready to tackle the questions below.

● Looking over the list of lies that you've identified, see which ones can be grouped together. For example, you may have internalized several lies related to a traumatic event in your life or as the result of a devastating loss.

● With your list in front of you, what's one of the biggest, most crippling lies you believe about yourself? Which one carries the most shame or emotional pain for you?

● How would you summarize the message perpetuating by the lies with the greatest hold on you? That you're not good enough? That no one would love you if they knew all your secrets? That you're not who you pretend to be? Something else?

- As you consider the lies you've identified, which ones work together to pull you down in certain areas? How does one lie often support another to bind your thinking?

- What strongholds have you identified based on recognizing the lies you've been believing? How would you describe the impact each of these strongholds is currently having on your life?

- While the goal is to demolish all of these mental strongholds, does one seem more urgent to you than others? Why? What step can you take to overcome this stronghold right away?

LESSON THREE

OLD LIES, NEW TRUTH

The definition of a principle is a decision you make once and then live by.

CRAIG GROESCHEL

I f you're going to demolish your strongholds, you have to recognize the power old lies have exercised in your thinking process. Many have become ingrained into your thought patterns without your awareness. Others you can identify, but they still persist and lead you astray. When you cling to these lies, you set yourself up to continue acting in ways that seem to reinforce their message.

For example, you crave close relationships with other people, longing to have them know you and accept you, flaws and all. Yet you've experienced enough rejection and disappointment in your life to know that it's a huge risk when you let down your guard and become vulnerable. Once you've had enough relationships fail to meet your hopes and expectations, you may assume that it's not worth the risk because no one will ever love you for who you are.

Or maybe you long to change careers and do something that would really make a positive difference, something that would excite you beyond the daily grind you experience now. But you tell yourself that it's too late, you're too old, and your opportunities for making dramatic career changes would be too costly. You accept that you might fail if you start over in a new, unfamiliar field, and then assume a worst-case scenario. Better to just play it safe and keep status quo.

It could be your finances and the burden of debt weighing you down. You've always had to live paycheck to paycheck so you believe that's the way it will always be. There doesn't seem to be any way to get out of debt and still live the way you're living now. But if you could just get out of debt, you know you could give generously and invest in ways that would make an eternal difference. Since you believe there's no way to live in financial peace, you believe that you're not cut out to be a giver.

These are just a few examples of the pervasive lies that get planted and cultivated over time based on self-fulfilling tendencies. You believe you can't do something so you don't really try. You assume your life will always be a certain way, so why bother trying to change. You've allowed the lies of the enemy to become the truth you live by.

And the devil is masterful when it comes to reinforcing beliefs that aren't true, false assumptions that become entrenched in how you think and behave. He exploits every opportunity to connect your life's pains, disappointments, and frustrations with negative, self-limiting beliefs. He basically convinces you to do his work for him by letting your imagination run wild in negative, cynical directions.

You've been held captive by the lies you believe for too long, and now it's time to take those lies captive to the divine power you have through Christ. With his help, you can capture the enemy's lies, pinpoint their origin, and uproot them from your thinking. It's time to go on the offensive against the devil's deceits in your mind.

Because God's truth can set you free.

EXPLORING GOD'S WORD

Your spiritual battle is made harder by the fact that you can't see your enemy. You don't realize the devil is the one leading you to believe these lies, which you probably didn't question at the time he planted them. But there was one time when this battle was *not* invisible, and it provides clear clues about how to wield God's massive power to demolish enemy-occupied strongholds.

After Jesus was baptized, he went into the desert to fast and pray for forty days and nights. It's no coincidence that Satan chose this time, when Jesus was alone and physically vulnerable, to tempt him. Take a look at the three ways the devil tried to get Jesus to believe a lie by putting a thin veneer of truth on it:

¹ Then Jesus was led by the Spirit into the wilderness to be tempted by the devil. ² After fasting forty days and forty nights, he was hungry. ³ The tempter came to him and said, "If you are the Son of God, tell these stones to become bread."

⁴ Jesus answered, "It is written: 'Man shall not live on bread alone, but on every word that comes from the mouth of God.'"

⁵ Then the devil took him to the holy city and had him stand on the highest point of the temple. ⁶ "If you are the Son of God," he said, "throw yourself down. For it is written:

> *"'He will command his angels concerning you,*
> *and they will lift you up in their hands,*
> *so that you will not strike your foot against a stone.'"*

⁷ Jesus answered him, "It is also written: 'Do not put the Lord your God to the test.'"

⁸ Again, the devil took him to a very high mountain and showed him all the kingdoms of the world and their splendor. ⁹ "All this I will give you," he said, "if you will bow down and worship me."

¹⁰ Jesus said to him, "Away from me, Satan! For it is written: 'Worship the Lord your God, and serve him only.'"

¹¹ Then the devil left him, and angels came and attended him.

– MATTHEW 4:1–11

- Why would the Spirit lead Jesus "into the wilderness to be tempted by the devil"? How did facing attacks from the enemy prepare Jesus for his earthly ministry?

- What are the three temptations Satan offers to Jesus when he's especially vulnerable? How does each one contain an element of truth based on a specific condition? Identify them here:

FIRST TEMPTATION:
Element of truth:

Vulnerability of Jesus:

SECOND TEMPTATION:
Element of truth:

Vulnerability of Jesus:

THIRD TEMPTATION:
Element of truth:

Vulnerability of Jesus:

- Why do you suppose Jesus refutes the devil each time by quoting from Scripture? What's the significance of responding this way?

- Does it surprise you that Satan also quotes from Scripture with his second temptation? Is he doing it just because Jesus did or for another reason?

- How does Satan attack Jesus' identity as the Son of God in each of these temptations? Why would the enemy focus on attacking Christ's identity?

- Why does the devil want to be worshiped as evidenced by his third temptation? How does worship relate to the way he's tempting Jesus here?

REFLECTING ON THE TRUTH

Ironically, one of the most important truths you must realize and accept is that the devil is a liar. His greatest weapon is deceit. In fact, lying may be the only weapon he can use against you. But he's often brilliant in pinpointing just how to use it.

Just consider the first glimpse we have of the devil in the Bible. What's he doing? Why, deceiving Adam and Eve in the garden, of course. In the form of the serpent, he created doubt in Eve's mind by asking her, "Did God really say, 'You must not eat from any tree in the garden'?" (Genesis 3:1). Then he lied to her: "You will not certainly die. . . . For God knows that when you eat from it your eyes will be opened, and you will be like God, knowing good and evil" (verses 4–5).

Notice how the devil uses questions to undermine truth here rather than attacking it directly. If he were direct and blatant, then his lies would be clearer and perhaps easier to resist. But he's crafty and knows just how to lie in ways that make it difficult to ignore.

Lying is what the devil does best and, just as he tempted Eve, he will tempt you to believe what's not true. The Bible explains, "But I am afraid that just as Eve was deceived by the serpent's cunning, your minds may somehow be led astray from your sincere and pure devotion to Christ" (2 Corinthians 11:3).

Part salesman, part con artist, part marketer, and part lawyer, Satan will whisper accusing questions and arrange deceptive statements to appear the way he wants you to see them. He schemes to twist your mind because if he can distract you from your purpose, drown out God's voice, and destroy your potential, then he can undermine the peace, joy, and purpose God has for you.

If the devil can get you to believe his lies, they will affect your life as if they were true.

- Looking back, when has the devil convinced you a lie was true in order to distort your thinking and lead you astray? How was he able to succeed at that time?

- Targeting Jesus when he was hungry, thirsty, and weary, the devil crafted temptations specifically aimed at these vulnerabilities. When are you especially vulnerable to listen to the enemy's lies and give in to temptation?

- Just as the serpent lied to Eve, the enemy knows how to make you feel like the exception to the rules and guidelines God has given us. Can you think of a time when you convinced yourself it was okay to sin based on the lies the devil planted in your thoughts? What was the result?

- Notice the way the devil shifted strategies each time he tempted Jesus in the wilderness. How have you experienced the enemy's cunning ability to bend the truth and get you to accept what you know is not true?

- In the past, how has the enemy caused you to question God and doubt what you know is true? What impact did this kind of questioning and doubting have on your faith?

- Sometimes the devil uses shame, exposure, and condemnation to plant his lies in our thinking. What's one of his emotionally charged lies that you continue to wrestle with? What makes this battle so challenging?

CHANGING YOUR STRATEGY

As you've experienced, Satan's lies are easy to believe. But his cunning is not the only reason you're often willing to believe them. Part of the spiritual battle in your mind results from the fact that you—like everyone else—have a flawed internal lie detector.

As imperfect human beings, we can't always see clearly and discern the truth. We're limited by our mortal perspective and by our own cognitive biases and past experiences. Remember, this spiritual battle is largely invisible because it's in our minds, even though the consequences play out in what we say, how we act, and what we do and don't do. The Bible warns us, "The heart is deceitful above all things and beyond cure" (Jeremiah 17:9), and, "There is a way that appears to be right, but in the end it leads to death" (Proverbs 14:12).

Learning to spot the devil's lies takes practice. Changing your strategy and winning the battle in your mind requires you to identify the enemy's lies in real time. After you've given in to temptation, said something you regret, or missed an opportunity because you played it safe, it's often easier to realize you listened to the devil's lies. Recognizing and overcoming them in the heat of the moment, however, relies on both defensive and offensive strategies. You'll focus more on offensive tactics in the next section and lessons to come, so use the questions below to help you create new, defensive strategies for protecting yourself.

- Based on past experiences, when are you especially vulnerable to the enemy's lies? Think about times you might be distracted, exhausted, or preoccupied in ways that leave you open to attack. Check all that apply and feel free to add your own:

  ____ when you're physically tired after work or exercise
  ____ when you're dealing with an ongoing problem at work
  ____ when you're in conflict with family members
  ____ when you're emotionally drained by a crisis or devastating event
  ____ when someone criticizes you in a way that feels harsh or unfair
  ____ when you feel rejected by someone you love, respect, and admire
  ____ when you're stressed about money, bills, and debt
  ____ when your normal daily routines are disrupted
  ____ when you're sick, injured, or battling a disease
  ____ when life seems to be going smoothly
  ____ when you're worried about your kids or other young family members
  ____ when you've just achieved a major goal or finished a big project
  ____ when you feel left out, lonely, or overlooked
  ____ when you're battling anxiety, fear, and depression
  ____ when you're forced to provide ongoing care for someone in need

____ when you're struggling in your faith or doubting God's presence in your life
____ when life's demands seem overwhelming

Other times:

Looking over the items you checked, think about how you can protect yourself from the enemy's lies in these times of low resistance. Then come up with tactics you can use during these particularly vulnerable times. For example, when you're feeling vulnerable because you're incredibly stressed at work, you might devise a plan of protection that looks like this:

- **Physical tactics:** eating healthy instead of junk food, drinking less caffeine, getting more sleep

- **Emotional tactics:** identifying why you feel stressed, confiding in a trusted friend, exercising strong boundaries

- **Spiritual tactics:** praying throughout your time at work, memorizing a Bible verse or passage on God's peace, asking others to pray for you

Okay, now it's your turn.

A TIME WHEN YOU'RE ESPECIALLY VULNERABLE:
Physical tactics for protection:

Emotional tactics for protection:

Spiritual tactics for protection:

ANOTHER TIME WHEN YOU'RE ESPECIALLY WEAK AND VULNERABLE:

Physical tactics for protection:

Emotional tactics for protection:

Spiritual tactics for protection:

AND ANOTHER TIME WHEN YOU'RE VULNERABLE:

Physical tactics for protection:

Emotional tactics for protection:

Spiritual tactics for protection:

EXERCISING THE EXCHANGE

As you know, relying on God's divine power is the only way to break strongholds and overcome the lies of the enemy. So along with defensive tactics, you can exercise the ultimate offensive tactic. Through the power of the Holy Spirit dwelling in you, it's possible to "be transformed by the renewing of your mind" (Romans 12:2).

Looking at this verse closely, the verb used is in the passive voice, meaning it is not something we *do*, but instead something that is *done to us*.

We have to be willing, though, and surrender our prideful way of doing things. We have to acknowledge our blind spots and remain vigilant during times when we're especially vulnerable. With God's help we can "take captive every thought to make it obedient to Christ" (2 Corinthians 10:5). We get out of our own way by no longer relying on our own power but instead trusting God and the victory we have in Christ.

When we're focused on him and his Word, God can renew our minds by leading us to "a knowledge of the truth" (2 Timothy 2:25). Immersed in his truth, we "come to [our] senses and escape from the trap of the devil, who has taken them captive to do his will" (2 Timothy 2:26). We're liberated to be all God created us to be because the battle in our minds is won! As Jesus said, "Then you will know the truth, and the truth will set you free" (John 8:32).

Shifting your attention from the devil's lies to God's truth, you focus on thoughts that strengthen, nourish, and empower your growth. This truth is found in God's Word. You'll build on this offensive strategy more in a later session, but for now come up with a verse, passage, or phrase from Scripture that directly addresses some of the false beliefs you've held and old lies you've accepted. Feel free to search online, use a concordance, or draw from passages you already know.

FALSE BELIEF:

Old lies supporting this belief:

Relevant truth from God's Word:

FALSE BELIEF:

Old lies supporting this belief:

Relevant truth from God's Word:

FALSE BELIEF:

Old lies supporting this belief:

Relevant truth from God's Word:

PART 2

THE REWIRE PRINCIPLE

REWIRE YOUR BRAIN, RENEW YOUR MIND

The reason you make poor decisions is because of how your brains works. Simply put, you have your wires crossed—we all do. So you need solutions that work in conjunction with the way your mind works. You have to not only recognize the unhealthy patterns but also figure out the underlying problem. If you want to win the war for your mind, you have to be willing to rewire your thought patterns and rewire the way your brain works. Then you can use the spiritual weapons God has given you to win the battles you face and fight daily.

As you practice the Rewire Principle, you will:

- Recognize the ways your neurological wires have gotten crossed based on the conditioning and repetition of past events.
- Identify the mental ruts that have become your default patterns for your thoughts and perspective.
- Understand how a trench of truth based on God's Word can change your thoughts.
- Create your own trench of truth that protects your mind and redirects your thoughts.
- Appreciate the importance of ruminating on God's Word in order to renew your mind.
- Learn to meditate and ruminate on truth from Scripture in order to redirect your thoughts and remind yourself that what God says is true.

CROSSED WIRES
AND CIRCULAR RUTS

If we want to win the war in our minds,
we have to be willing to rewire our thought patterns, rewire our brains.

CRAIG GROESCHEL

Remember when you learned to swim or ride a bike, to drive a car or play a musical instrument? The first time you tried these new activities, you probably made lots of mistakes and missteps. Over time, though, as you repeated the steps the new activity required, you gradually improved. As you think about what you're learning and doing it again and again, you master the ability to perform it without the same levels of exertion.

Activities like these often involve complex motor skills, requiring coordination of different sensory input, especially what you're seeing and hearing, with muscle alignment. New drivers usually grip the steering wheel with both hands. New bikers think about peddling with their feet while steering with their hands. Playing the guitar or keyboard requires learning to use your fingers and hands in ways synchronized with visual data, the musical notes on the page, with auditory data, the sounds the keys and chords make in sequence.

Every thought, regardless of how you evaluate it, produces a neurochemical change in your mind. Your brain literally redesigns itself around that thought. Like a complex command center, your brain activates the parts of your body through neurons. As neurons link together to create messages, over time they create neural pathways. The presence of a neural pathway makes it easier to think that thought or for your body to send that same message again.

Simply put, neural pathways are brain ruts.

The more you do something, the more natural it becomes because you form neural pathways in your brain. Thinking a thought or taking an action will go from difficult to easy. With enough repetition, it will become automatic to fall into that neurological rut. You don't have to think about every single step in the process the way you did when you first started.

Obviously, neural pathways help you master complex activities or multi-task in order to accomplish more sometimes. Repetition formed helpful ruts. Your brain seems to automatically know what to do as you swim, bike, drive, or play a song.

But neural pathways can also create problems. In fact, the reason you, along with everyone else, tend to make irrational, self-defeating decisions over and over is because the same neural pathways that help you improve performance of certain tasks also reinforces bad habits as well.

Your neural ruts are often carved deeper by the bundle of nerves at the base of your brainstem known as the Reticular Activating System (RAS). The RAS sifts and filters through millions of pieces of sensory data being sent to your brain and groups them according to relevance and similarity. If the info will keep you alive, prevent problems, avert danger, or bring pleasure, then the RAS is on it. But it's more sophisticated than just primary needs because this system also explains why that new app you just downloaded is suddenly on everyone's lips, why you notice red Hondas like your new one everywhere, and why you can't help hearing someone call your name in a crowd.

Our RAS also utilizes our established beliefs to screen incoming data points. Which explains why we tend to get what we expect so much of the time. If you tell yourself that you're a victim who never has a steady job and long-lasting relationships, then you condition your brain to reinforce these beliefs. You train yourself to assume the worst and then do what it takes to maintain that belief by the way you interpret new experiences.

Being "in a rut" is a common cliché, but it's more literally true than you might imagine. Repeated thoughts create paths in your brain. As these thoughts create belief systems, the rut gets deeper. Pretty soon, you feel stuck in a cycle that you can't break.

Paying attention and being deliberate about how you respond to your thoughts, however, can help you break out of your ruts and make lasting changes. If you want to win the battle for your mind, you need a solution that works with the way your brain works. You need a way to rewire your thought patterns in order to eliminate old ruts and establish new pathways.

EXPLORING GOD'S WORD

You are always creating and falling into neurological ruts. God designed your brain to work this way so that you smoothly, even automatically, create and develop habits. Your brain's way of working helps you develop healthy habits like brushing your teeth or doing laundry, but it also reinforces destructive, harmful thought patterns that develop from your experiences.

For instance, the hit of dopamine you got from experiencing pleasure when you ate a hot, glazed donut can lead you to eating more of them when you're feeling sad or lonely. The feelings stirred when viewing porn or shopping online create a message that this kind of pleasure provides comfort and relief when you're bored, disappointed, or anxious. Depending on a number of variables, especially circumstances and emotional context, your brain creates neural pathways that you attach to certain patterns, which in turn keep you stuck in a rut going around in circles.

This process explains how addictions form and bad habits haunt us. We try to avoid pain and to seek pleasure as we navigate our way through the daily events of our lives. Even when we don't like what we're doing and actively try to break the cycle, we often feel powerless and frustrated, much like what Paul described in Romans 7:15–24.

Many people in the Bible illustrate patterns of repetitive, unhealthy behavior, including Jacob and his deceptive tricks, Moses and his temper, and Naomi with her worst-case complaints. But one in particular, identified only as a Samaritan woman, reveals not only the default tendency to keep making the same self-defeating choices but the only way to break the cycle.

[7] When a Samaritan woman came to draw water, Jesus said to her, "Will you give me a drink?" [8] (His disciples had gone into the town to buy food.)

[9] The Samaritan woman said to him, "You are a Jew and I am a Samaritan woman. How can you ask me for a drink?" (For Jews do not associate with Samaritans.)

[10] Jesus answered her, "If you knew the gift of God and who it is that asks you for a drink, you would have asked him and he would have given you living water."

[11] "Sir," the woman said, "you have nothing to draw with and the well is deep. Where can you get this living water? [12] Are you greater than our father Jacob, who gave us the well and drank from it himself, as did also his sons and his livestock?"

[13] Jesus answered, "Everyone who drinks this water will be thirsty again, [14] but whoever drinks the water I give them will never thirst. Indeed, the water I give them will become in them a spring of water welling up to eternal life."

[15] The woman said to him, "Sir, give me this water so that I won't get thirsty and have to keep coming here to draw water."

[16] He told her, "Go, call your husband and come back."

[17] "I have no husband," she replied.

Jesus said to her, "You are right when you say you have no husband. [18] The fact is, you have had five husbands, and the man you now have is not your husband. What you have just said is quite true."

— JOHN 4:7–18

- What assumption does the woman make when Jesus asks her for a drink of water? How are our responses to others often the result of neural pathways we've formed based on our life experiences, cultural contexts, and social biases?

- How does Jesus shift their conversation from cultural differences to something all people have in common? Why did this shift likely surprise the Samaritan woman?

- Why does the Samaritan woman struggle to realize Jesus is speaking metaphorically about spiritual thirst? Why might she be blinded to her spiritual need based on her past relationships?

- Jesus clearly knows about this woman's life and the numerous husbands she has had, yet why do you suppose he doesn't confront her directly? Is he implying there's a connection between her spiritual thirst and her numerous relationships with men?

By the end of her conversation with Jesus, this woman realizes he is the anticipated Messiah. She told others in her community about her encounter, and they also believed and invited Jesus and his disciples to stay with them. As you can see, her testimony not only reflected the way her life had changed but became a catalyst for change in the lives of those around her:

> [39] *Many of the Samaritans from that town believed in him because of the woman's testimony, "He told me everything I ever did."* [40] *So when the Samaritans came to him, they urged him to stay with them, and he stayed two days.* [41] *And because of his words many more became believers.*
>
> [42] *They said to the woman, "We no longer believe just because of what you said; now we have heard for ourselves, and we know that this man really is the Savior of the world."*
>
> – JOHN 4:39–42

- How did meeting Jesus become a turning point in this woman's life? How did her conversation with him turn her expectations about her life inside out?

- After encountering the Messiah, do you think this woman related differently to men? Why?

REFLECTING ON THE TRUTH

Perhaps it was just coincidence that the Samaritan woman had five previous husbands and was living with a man not her husband when she met Jesus at the well that day. The implication, however, is that she had come to rely on men without being able to fully commit and remain married. They may have all been terrible men, and she may have been justified in dissolving each union to pursue the next. But if that were true, then she was still caught in a cycle of choosing poorly and repeating her mistakes.

We all get caught in ruts and behave in ways that we know are not good for us. Some habits we do on autopilot without even realizing it, such as checking our phones and scrolling social media every free minute. Other ruts lead us to areas that are uniquely and distinctly our own, based on our past experiences, relationships, and the consequences of our choices. We start to believe that we're victims of our circumstances and become passive in exercising choices that would help us change course. We quit trying because it feels futile and too frustrating.

Without an intentional decision to break the pattern, your life will continue moving in the wrong direction. It's normal. It's easy. It's the same old rut. But like the Samaritan woman, you're not without hope. You simply have to realize that your ruts can never satisfy your soul. Most of the time, they will leave you even thirstier than before.

- How do you relate to the Samaritan woman in her conversation with Jesus? In what specific ways?

- What surprises you most about Jesus' conversation with the Samaritan woman? Why?

- How often are you aware of your own biases when it comes to other people? What are some of the ways you stereotype others or allow cultural expectations to shape your interactions?

- If you had been in this situation like the Samaritan woman, with Jesus knowing everything about your life, what habit or rut might he have mentioned? Instead of referencing her five husbands and current roommate, what specific example would Jesus include from your life?

- When have you recently found yourself doing something you knew you didn't want to do? Looking back now, how do you regard this incident—a minor frustration that you can control if you want to, or an ongoing battle against an ingrained habit that seems to have a life of its own?

- How do your ruts prevent you from growing closer to God and other people? When have you noticed this most recently?

CHANGING YOUR STRATEGY

Some ruts develop in your life from positive experiences or initially good habits that turn negative when you become fixated on them or rely on them for security, comfort, and control. Several of the examples in chapter 4 of *Winning the War in Your Mind* demonstrate the way something begins harmlessly enough, such as hearing your grandmother talk about hard times and the importance of saving money, but turns destructive when you obsess or make something, like being frugal and saving money, into an idol.

You likely have similar neural ruts that developed as the result of an experience, conversation, or intense feeling, which were then reinforced over time as you relied on them. As you're learning, in order to break the automatic flow of these behavior patterns, you have to be aware of them and be deliberate in your strategy to redirect them. One way to uncross your crossed neural wires involves not only identifying your trouble areas but analyzing each one so you can trace its development. You may not be able to know how or why some deep-rooted habits formed, but you might be surprised at what you learn when you step back and study your own behavior patterns.

Building on exercise 7, "Recognizing Your Ruts," in chapter 4 in the book, spend a few minutes examining the behaviors, actions, tendencies, and preferences that are hindering your progress in the battle for your mind. Fill in the blanks in each of the statements below to aid in your time of rut identification and reflection.

One rut that affects my life on a daily basis is _____

_____ .

During the day, I probably get stuck in this rut when I feel _____ or wish that _____ .

A negative habit or tendency I've held onto since childhood is _____
_____ .

It probably began when _____
because _____ .

The neural rut or harmful habit I'm most ashamed of struggling with has to be _____
_____ .

I feel it's the worst because _____ .

If you asked my family and closest friends about the mental ruts and behavior habits that trip me up, they would say _____ .

The habit, behavior, or addiction I've battled the longest is probably _____
_____ .

When I think about times I've tried to change or kick old habits, I feel like _____
_____ .

The main reason my past efforts to change these habits has failed is because _____
_____ .

EXERCISING THE EXCHANGE

One of the most effective ways of changing mental ruts is by creating a trench of truth, which you'll learn about in the next book chapter and workbook session. Before you create your truth trench, however, it often helps to soften the ground by praying over the spiritual soil you're cultivating. You may also find encouragement by reading what Jesus said regarding the process of spiritual growth and making it a part of your prayer:

[1] *"I am the true vine, and my Father is the gardener.* [2] *He cuts off every branch in me that bears no fruit, while every branch that does bear fruit he prunes so that it will be even more fruitful.* [3] *You are already clean because of the word I have spoken to you.* [4] *Remain in me, as I also remain in you. No branch can bear fruit by itself; it must remain in the vine. Neither can you bear fruit unless you remain in me.*

[5] *"I am the vine; you are the branches. If you remain in me and I in you, you will bear much fruit; apart from me you can do nothing.* [6] *If you do not remain in me, you are like a branch that is thrown away and withers; such branches are picked up, thrown into the fire and burned.* [7] *If you remain in me and my words remain in you, ask whatever you wish, and it will be done for you.* [8] *This is to my Father's glory, that you bear much fruit, showing yourselves to be my disciples."*

— JOHN 15:1–8

Read these words Jesus shared with his followers once again, slowly and out loud. As you begin praying over specific ruts and behaviors you want to change, invite God's Spirit to speak directly to your heart through these words. Here's a prayer to get you started, but feel free to add to it, personalize it, and make it your own:

Father, I know there are branches in my life that aren't bearing fruit, or at least not bearing fruit like they should. I want to serve you and love you fully, Lord, so remove those branches as I seek to break out of the mental ruts that have been keeping me stuck, stagnant, and dissatisfied with my life. I know that true life is only found as I abide in Christ and grow through the power of your Spirit dwelling in me. I'm ready to surrender all areas of my life to you now. I want to win the war in my mind because I know you created me for a greater purpose than I've been pursuing. Give me strength, wisdom, and hope, God, as I do my part to allow your supernatural power to change me from the inside out. Amen.

CREATING A TRENCH OF TRUTH

To stop the lies and replace them with truth, we need to look to God's Word.

CRAIG GROESCHEL

Too often, most people focus on changing their behavior by making a commitment to start doing this or stop doing that. You've likely experienced this before when you've made a New Year's resolution to read your Bible daily, vowed to quit smoking cold turkey, or promised yourself to exercise and eat healthy food. But how's that worked out for you?

The problem with attacking your problem is that you focus on the problem. Behavior modification doesn't work because it focuses on, well, modifying behavior. It doesn't get to the root of the problem, which is the thought that produces the behavior, the false beliefs entrenched in your mind. More specifically, the problem is the neural pathway that led to the behavior.

If you stop a behavior it will likely come back unless you remove the lie at the root of the behavior and replace the neural pathway that leads to the behavior.

As you continue capturing the lies in your thoughts and replacing them with truth, now it's time to explore closing old destructive neural ruts and creating new helpful ones. The antidote for a negative neural pathway is a new positive neural pathway. Instead of living in a rut, you create a truth trench that runs deeper, diverting the flow of thoughts away from old pathways and into new ones.

For example, you have a series of thoughts you set in motion each time you're triggered by events, images, people, memories, and your senses. Your trigger might be feeling lonely, or fearing rejection, or overhearing others enjoying themselves. Once triggered, you fall into the same series of thoughts you always fall into, and they lead to the same behavior.

To break this pattern so that your triggers don't automatically send you into your default behaviors, you're going to strategically choose a new series of thoughts. To stop the lies and replace them with truth you need to look to God's Word because that's the weapon God gives you for the battle you're fighting. His truth has the power to set you free, and you are going to choose specific Bible verses to create a new neural pathway that applies directly to your problem.

For this to work, though, you need more than just to *know* God's Word; you'll want to internalize it, to have it sink deep within your being as part of you. The author of Psalm 119 expressed this concept this way: "I have hidden your word in my heart that I might not sin against you" (verse 11).

Based on the truth of God's Word related to your areas of struggle, you can create declarations to counter the old neural ruts and to establish new ones. As you draw your declarations from God's truth, you can then custom tailor them to your particular battles and behaviors. With practice, patience, and perseverance, your declarations will replace those old default neural pathways and create deep channels focused on God's truth instead. If you want to win the war for your mind, then you must claim the victory you already have in Christ and create a neural pathway that reinforces your victory.

EXPLORING GOD'S WORD

What we put in our minds comes out in our lives. But much of the time, we rarely pay attention to all that we allow into our minds. In fact, we're constantly bombarded by thoughts triggered by information seemingly outside our control.

Psychological studies reveal that we may face hundreds of unintentional and intrusive thoughts each day, many resulting from the messages we receive and interpret from social media, advertising, and online data.

Psychologists who conduct these studies often point to the "law of exposure," which says that your mind absorbs and reflects what it is exposed to the most. Basically, if you allow a thought into your mind it will come out in your life. The famous philosopher and mathematician René Descartes is credited with the phrase "I think, therefore I am," but evidence and experience reveal that it might be more accurately said, "*What* I think, therefore I am."

Paul likely had this in mind when he wrote, "Those who are dominated by the sinful nature think about sinful things, but those who are controlled by the Holy Spirit think about things that please the Spirit. So letting your sinful nature control your mind leads to death. But letting the Spirit control your mind leads to life and peace" (Romans 8:5-6 NLT).

Paul is teaching us that if you allow a thought into your mind it will come out in your life. So, if you want to change your life, you have to change your thinking. You'll want to shift from old lies and false assumptions to God's timeless truth. God's Word transforms your thinking and equips you to capture thoughts, resist the enemy, and remain centered on truth. This is not a new revelation but one taught throughout Scripture, including the Psalms. As you read through the following passage, underline or circle the words, phrases, and images that emphasize the importance of focusing on God's truth.

[1] *Blessed are those whose ways are blameless,*
who walk according to the law of the LORD.
[2] *Blessed are those who keep his statutes*
and seek him with all their heart—
[3] *they do no wrong*
but follow his ways.
[4] *You have laid down precepts*
that are to be fully obeyed.
[5] *Oh, that my ways were steadfast*
in obeying your decrees!
[6] *Then I would not be put to shame*
when I consider all your commands.

⁷ *I will praise you with an upright heart*
 as I learn your righteous laws.
⁸ *I will obey your decrees;*
 do not utterly forsake me.

⁹ *How can a young person stay on the path of purity?*
 By living according to your word.
¹⁰ *I seek you with all my heart;*
 do not let me stray from your commands.
¹¹ *I have hidden your word in my heart*
 that I might not sin against you.
¹² *Praise be to you, LORD;*
 teach me your decrees.
¹³ *With my lips I recount*
 all the laws that come from your mouth.
¹⁴ *I rejoice in following your statutes*
 as one rejoices in great riches.
¹⁵ *I meditate on your precepts*
 and consider your ways.
¹⁶ *I delight in your decrees;*
 I will not neglect your word.

— PSALM 119:1–16

- What are some of the words the psalmist uses to reference God's truth in this passage? List them here and what you think of or associate with each one.

- According to the psalmist, what are some of the many benefits of studying and obeying God's decrees, commands, statutes, and precepts? Which benefit especially resonates or hits home with you?

- What does the psalmist imply typically happens to those who fail to study and follow God's laws?

- Review the words, phrases, and images you underlined or circled. What unique attributes of God's truth do these reveal and describe? Which word, phrase, or image stands out most to you?

- How does hiding God's word in one's heart (see verse 11) help strengthen the speaker's desire to resist sin and to obey God?

- Based on this passage, why do you suppose praise and worship are natural consequences of studying God's Word?

REFLECTING ON THE TRUTH

Whether you've been reading and studying the Bible all your life or it's a new pursuit, reflecting on God's truth is essential to winning the war in your mind. If studying and applying the Word is a struggle in itself, then it's important to pause for a moment to consider what's going on. Because immersing yourself in God's Word is vitally important to your personal and spiritual growth and the victory you want to have in your mind.

So begin by thinking about your relationship to the Bible. Maybe you've heard so many different, conflicting viewpoints on various passages that you're uncertain how to read and understand Scripture. You might feel intimidated by words, phrases, names, and places that are new and unfamiliar. Perhaps your way of reading and studying the Bible relies on neural ruts that developed as a result of what and how you were taught about it as a child. You have matured and grown since then, however, and are more equipped to experience a deeper understanding.

Whatever your past relationship with God's Word, it's time to recognize it as your supernatural power source of strength, wisdom, and instruction. Use the questions below to help you reflect on what you can do to approach the Bible with a new appreciation for its role in your life.

- How much were you exposed to the Bible as a child? What role did it have in your upbringing?

- What are some misperceptions or inaccurate beliefs about Scripture that you've had to overcome? How did these negative assumptions originate?

- On a scale of 1 to 10, with 1 being "rarely if ever" and 10 being "every day," how often do you read or listen to the Bible? When was the last time you spent at least ten minutes studying something in Scripture?

- What intimidates or frustrates you most about studying your Bible? What do you enjoy most about spending time in the Word?

- How has your appreciation of God's Word increased or changed over the course of your life? Why?

● What Bible verse or passage holds special meaning in your life right now? Why is it so important to you?

CHANGING YOUR STRATEGY

As you've learned by now, you must be diligent about what you allow into your mind. Because the thoughts that consume your mind also control your life. Your negative thoughts have created unhealthy neural pathways, but you don't have to remain stuck in the ruts they've formed. You can expose old lies and create positive, God-honoring pathways that form new neural grooves that provide a trench of truth around your mind.

The way you do this is by meditating on the truths from God's Word that apply to your mental battles. If meditation sounds scary or unsettling, you should remember two things: (1) meditation is simply focusing your thoughts deliberately for a sustained period of time; and (2) the Bible talks about meditating a lot—on God's goodness and on his Word.

Clearly, this kind of God-focused meditation is different from most Eastern meditation practices with a goal of emptying your mind. Christian meditation is filling your mind with God's truth. It is being strategic and deliberate about what you allow into your mind. It's about making the law of exposure work for you instead of against you. It's mastering your mind by creating a solution for your mental ruts that work with the way your brain works.

While you will practice several ways to meditate this way, one effective strategy for winning the war for your mind is a declaration of victory based on God's truth. For each of the various negative ruts you've identified, you can create a declaration that counters the lies and false beliefs of that old neural pathway. The process is simple but not necessarily easy to put in practice.

First, choose one particular pattern of negative thinking to correct. For example, you might address the way your internal thoughts always seem to criticize what you say or do in front of other people. No matter how well-spoken you may be or how much others seem to appreciate and enjoy what you do, your thoughts hold you to an impossible standard. But no longer!

After you focus on a particular rut, then you want to dig your trench of truth by collecting verses and passages from the Bible that relate to this problem area. So in order to combat your destructive, self-critical, perfectionistic, never-good-enough thoughts, you might select verses such as these:

I praise you because I am fearfully and wonderfully made;
your works are wonderful,
I know that full well.

— PSALM 139:14

If God is for us, who can be against us? . . . We are more than conquerors through him who loved us.

— ROMANS 8:31, 37

I can do all this through him who gives me strength.

— PHILIPPIANS 4:13

There are many more verses and passages you might collect, but you get the idea. Whatever thematic topic and issues you're countering, choose truth based on what God says about it to replace the old lies.

Now it's your turn. While eventually you will create declarations to replace all the negative ruts, start with the one that's currently disrupting your life the most.

Negative rut to replace:

Thoughts that support and reinforce this rut with lies:

What God's Word says about this subject:

Bible verses and passages that relate:

EXERCISING THE EXCHANGE

Armed with the truth of God's Word on the matter you've identified from your negative rut, now it's time to draft your declaration. Remember, the goal is to meditate on what God says is true by saturating your mind. Your declaration helps you saturate your thinking as you write it, think it, and confess it until its truth becomes your bedrock belief.

As templates or reference points, review the examples in the section titled "Determining Declarations" in chapter 5 of *Winning the War for Your Mind*. Notice the way a declaration is written in first-person ("When I am. . ." and "God is for me . . .") within the context of truth revealed by your Scripture verses and passages. Write your declaration as if it is already true, even if you're not sure it is or don't fully believe it yet. The goal here is simply to claim the victory you have in Jesus Christ by creating a neural pathway reinforcing this truth.

Keep in mind that you should be creative and make this declaration your own. Spend some time in prayer as you put together your affirmation of truth to replace the destructive lies that have damaged your thinking long enough. Don't get hung up on grammar, spelling, or poetic expression. Make it direct, clear, concise, and focused on you and God.

MY DECLARATION ON _____

Scripture references included:

First draft:

Final draft:

RUMINATION AND RENEWAL

*Meditating is taking a thought—in our case a Bible verse or
a declaration based on God's Word—and chewing on it, then swallowing it,
then bringing it back to mind and chewing on it some more.*

CRAIG GROESCHEL

Have you noticed that the devil keeps whispering the same lies to you? He has repeatedly been whispering the same lies to you your entire life because he knows the more often you think a thought, the more likely you are to believe it and for it to become a rut you get stuck in. Simply put, the devil goes all in on one strategy: Repetition is the reason for ruts.

If you consider your greatest areas of struggle, you can likely see evidence of how the enemy is stuck in the same loop of lies. He is repetitive, not creative. If he were creative, today he'd tempt you to argue with your spouse and tomorrow with someone else, but he usually chooses his targets and sticks with them, using the same strategies to attack your vulnerable areas over and over again. He knows if he tells you a lie often enough, you will believe it.

To overcome his lies, you're going to replace his loop with a trench of truth. You're going to craft a declaration drawn from God's Word and then focus on it until it soaks until your soul. You're going to utilize the same method the enemy uses so effectively—repetition.

God tells us to meditate on his Word repeatedly—just check out the evidence in the next section. In each verse urging you to meditate, the word used essentially means ruminate. It's not very pretty, and may in fact be downright gross, but ruminate literally means to chew over and over and over again, like cows do with their cud. They get a mouthful of grass, chew it up, swallow it, *throw it back up in their mouths*, chew it some more, swallow it again, and keep going back and forth like this over and over again.

That is also the essence of *meditate*. Meditating is taking a thought—in our case a Bible verse or a declaration we have written—and chewing on it, then swallowing it, then bringing it back to our minds and chewing on it some more. Then we swallow it again, then bring it back to our minds and chew on it more. We do that over and over and over, meditating on God's truth and God's love and God's great deeds because it allows us to get the maximum amount of spiritual nutrition out of our godly thoughts.

As you chew on God's Word and digest his truth, you change the way you think. As you repeat this process of meditation, or thought rumination if you prefer, you create new neural pathways. Old negative ruts get replaced with new trenches of truth.

Ruminate, digest, repeat.

Write it, think it, confess it, believe it.

Over and over and over and over and over again and again . . .

This will take some work. It will not be easy. But if you do persevere, you will create new neural trenches founded on truth. God will renew your mind.

And when you renew your mind, you live in freedom.

EXPLORING GOD'S WORD

When the Bible tells us to meditate on who God is, what he's done, and what his Word says, it conveys an ongoing sense of reflecting, pondering, questioning, studying, comprehending, obeying, and, yes, chewing. This kind of engagement requires more from you—more attention, more focus, more connection—than you may be used to exercising. Like most people, you probably read bits and pieces of information throughout your day, from news that scrolls on your phone screen to reports and documents related to work, from emails and texts from friends and family to pop-up ads in articles and games.

In a world of sound bites, memes, and tweets, it can be challenging to focus in an undistracted way on just one thing. But this is what meditating and ruminating on God's truth requires if you're going to create new neural pathways and win the war for your mind. Like the scalpel of a surgeon and the weapon of a warrior, God's Word has the ability to heal your mind as well as protect it from assaults by the enemy: "For the word of God is alive and active. Sharper than any double-edged sword, it penetrates even to dividing soul and spirit, joints and marrow; it judges the thoughts and attitudes of the heart" (Hebrews 4:12).

In order to access this kind of power, though, you must be immersed and soaked in its truth. You'll want to fill your thoughts with an eternal perspective instead of a temporary glance. You consider what it means to obey God by stepping out in faith even when you don't understand your limited view of circumstances. You dwell on God's thoughts instead of your own, living by faith and relying on the power of his Spirit.

As you consider what this looks like for you, read through the following verses and passages. Place an X or star beside the one or two that speak to your heart the most right now. Underline any words or phrases that jump out at you. Look for connections—of language, ideas, images—shared among these different statements. Then answer the questions that follow as you prepare to put their messages into practice.

Keep this Book of the Law always on your lips; meditate on it day and night, so that you may be careful to do everything written in it. Then you will be prosperous and successful.

— JOSHUA 1:8

[1] Blessed is the one
    who does not walk in step with the wicked
or stand in the way that sinners take
    or sit in the company of mockers,
[2] but whose delight is in the law of the LORD,
    and who meditates on his law day and night.

³ *That person is like a tree planted by streams of water,*
        which yields its fruit in season
and whose leaf does not wither—
        whatever they do prospers.

— PSALM 1:1-3

⁹ *Within your temple, O God,*
        we meditate on your unfailing love.

— PSALM 48:9

¹² *I will consider all your works*
        and meditate on all your mighty deeds.

— PSALM 77:12

²³ *Though rulers sit together and slander me,*
        your servant will meditate on your decrees.
²⁴ *Your statutes are my delight;*
        they are my counselors.

— PSALM 119:23–24

²⁶ *I gave an account of my ways and you answered me;*
        teach me your decrees.
²⁷ *Cause me to understand the way of your precepts,*
        that I may meditate on your wonderful deeds.

— PSALM 119:26–27

⁵ *I remember the days of long ago;*
        I meditate on all your works
        and consider what your hands have done.

— PSALM 143:5

⁵ *They speak of the glorious splendor of your majesty—*
        and I will meditate on your wonderful works.

— PSALM 145:5

- What is the focal point of each speaker/writer's meditation? Make a list of the specific things mentioned that involve meditation according to each verse or passage.

- Based on these verses, what role does memory play in meditation? What role do you think it plays?

- What are the consequences of meditation according to these verses? How does meditation produce blessings in and of itself?

- What characteristics of God are worthy of meditation here? Why are these qualities important to understand and appreciate in your relationship with God?

- How does meditation differ from prayer based on how it's described in these various verses? And how is meditation similar to prayer?

● With these verses in mind, how would you describe the connection between meditation and obedience regarding your relationship with God?

REFLECTING ON THE TRUTH

In order to reflect on God's truth through meditation, you will also want to work on removing distractions, disruptions, and diversions. In our online world of 24–7 connectivity, this is harder than you may think. If you're like most people, you've grown accustomed to checking texts, emails, and up-to-the-minute news frequently throughout your day. When you're not working or responding to others, then you probably rely on your phone to entertain you with apps, games, podcasts, ebooks, videos, music, and TV shows and movies.

Generally speaking, more sources compete for your attention than ever before. And it's tough to unplug and ignore your phone or online device. The fear of missing out (FOMO) is very real for people who like being aware of every possible variable, both personal and public, affecting them. You may or may not be one of them, but regardless you are wise to practice another trait that goes hand in hand with meditation: solitude.

Repeatedly in Scripture, people left their routines and communities in order to be alone with God. Jesus frequently stepped away from his disciples and the crowds following him in order to pray and commune with his Heavenly Father. It's not that God is somewhere else that he and others have to venture to in order to find God—more likely, it's about removing the clamor of daily life and the pull of other people.

Spend a few minutes thinking about what consumes your attention on an average day. Use these questions to help you reflect on what it means for you to quiet yourself before God in order to focus on him and only him. Because eliminating unnecessary drains on your time and energy will give you more of both to meditate on God and his truth.

- What's the biggest consumer of your attention in the course of a normal day? Keep in mind that just because you spend a lot of time doing something it doesn't mean you're engaged or paying attention.

- What are some of the ways you know you waste time in a given day? Check all that apply and add others that come to mind:

_____ scrolling news on my phone
_____ texting with friends and acquaintances about non-important matters
_____ watching funny memes to share with others
_____ listening to podcasts, music, or audiobooks
_____ talking to others about current events and pop culture
_____ watching sports
_____ playing games online
_____ taking selfies
_____ daydreaming about nothing in particular
_____ worrying about things you can't control
_____ replaying conversations you've already had and analyzing what was said
_____ viewing images online that you know you shouldn't
_____ napping, dozing, or mindlessly watching YouTube

Other time-wasters:

- When was the last time you unplugged and spent time alone with God? What were the circumstances and how could you improve them to focus more intently?

- What are some ways you can eliminate or at least reduce interruptions when you're meditating and focusing on God?

- When and where is a good time and place for you to spend time alone with God? What do you need to change to make this happen?

- Review some of the negative, destructive thought ruts you experience on a regular basis. Try to identify usual triggers for each one. How can you now use these triggers to shift your attention to God and meditate on your declarations of his truth?

CHANGING YOUR STRATEGY

Instead of slipping into negative thoughts and sinking into mental ruts, you want to develop the habit of focusing on God, his truth, and your relationship with him as much as possible. Over time, the more you meditate, the more you don't have to think about doing it and the less mental effort it requires. Because your goal is to make meditating a matter of automaticity.

Automaticity is the ability to do things without thinking about each individual action or task required to complete what you are doing. It's when repetition allows an action to become an automatic response. Most likely, you experience automaticity when you take a shower, drive your car to work, or clean up the kitchen after a meal. You don't consciously think about each separate act necessary to complete your overall goal. You just start doing what's necessary, allowing your brain to go on autopilot in conjunction with your body's sense memory.

Automaticity is also why you keep doing things you *don't* want to do. Repetition has led to it becoming an automatic, default kind of response. Your goal now is to break those destructive automatic behaviors by meditating on God's Word and on your declarations. The truth of what God says becomes your new automaticity.

You want to make falling into the right rut, which in turn leads you to the right thoughts and actions, automatic. It's the idea at the heart of the old axiom, "Watch your thoughts, they become your words; watch your words, they become your actions; watch your actions, they become your habits; watch your habits, they become your character; watch your character, it becomes your destiny."

If you haven't done it already, now is the time to craft your declarations based on God's Word to replace your negative thought storms. If you struggle to find time to meditate, then write a declaration about how your time on earth is a gift from God that you want to use wisely. Whatever your areas of struggle, take the time to create declarations for each one that you can use to focus your meditations and anchor your attention.

MY DECLARATION ON _____

Scripture references included:

First draft:

Final draft:

MY DECLARATION ON _____

Scripture references included:

First draft:

Final draft:

EXERCISING THE EXCHANGE

Don't be discouraged if meditating regularly makes you feel awkward or anxious. When you're used to having something, usually many things, consume your attention all the time, it's often unsettling and unfamiliar to calm down and focus singularly. So expect establishing a meditation habit to feel uncomfortable at first.

After all, you've been thinking the same thoughts and doing the same things for years. It will take time to replace those neural pathways. But don't give up. Keep moving forward. You will probably take a step forward and then a step back. Two steps forward, one step back. Slowly but surely, you will discover that your thoughts don't go dark by default but instead shine with the light of God's truth.

As you persevere in your new practice, it's often good to get creative. To help you pursue automaticity in your meditation and thought patterns, choose at least one of the following three exercises to saturate your mind in God's Word, in thanksgiving for all he's done for you, and in absorbing your declarations.

- **Exercise 1:** If you know how to speak or read a foreign language, then you know that a good translation requires both accuracy and style. For this exercise, translate one of your declarations into another language of your choice. Obviously, if you're fluent in a language other than English, this exercise will be easier. But even if you don't speak Spanish, Mandarin, or Italian, you can still use online translation tools to assist you. Once you have your declaration translated, practice saying it out loud. Speaking it in another language will force you to slow down and think about what you're actually saying.

- **Exercise 2:** Choose one of your declarations and take it on a walk or hike. Regardless of your fitness level or the distance you cover, try to go at a natural pace that will allow you to focus most of your attention on the meaning of your declaration. As you walk or hike, try to memorize your declaration by breaking it down into shorter phrases that you can master before adding the next one. Focus on the meaning of each key phrase as you commit it to memory before adding the next phrase.

- **Exercise 3**: This exercise involves finding a visual way to illustrate your declaration. You might especially enjoy this if you're creative or crafty, but you don't have to be an artist to fulfill it successfully. The goal is for you to reflect on how to translate the language of your declaration into images, symbols, and graphic expressions. You can doodle, sketch, paint, embroider, sculpt, or sew your visual declaration, and no one else needs to understand it necessarily. The goal is simply for you to spend time focused on God's truth in a way that includes language but also includes color, texture, dimension, and scale. Have fun with this one!

PART 3

THE REFRAME PRINCIPLE

REFRAME YOUR MIND, RESTORE YOUR PERSPECTIVE

As you learn more about how your brain works, you will realize the incredible ability you have to reframe your thinking and literally redesign your mind around new thoughts. Part of the problem is that you, along with everyone else, have cognitive biases that create blind spots and prejudice your perspective of what you're seeing and interpreting around you. That's why it's so important to think about what you think about. You cannot correct a problem you don't recognize or defeat an enemy you cannot define.

As you practice the Reframe Principle, you will:

- Realize the way your past experiences and habits create cognitive bias and reinforce mental ruts.
- Identify your own cognitive biases and learn to reframe your perspective on your experiences.
- Praise God for what he didn't do that you requested, trusting more fully that he knows what's best for you and your life.
- Reflect on the benefits and blessings of your past unanswered prayers.
- Discover how to see God's goodness at work despite your circumstances and feelings.
- Foster a habit of looking for God's goodness at work in your life on a daily basis.

LENSES AND FILTERS

*You cannot control what's happened or what will happen,
but you can control how you perceive it.*

CRAIG GROESCHEL

How often do you see what you *expect* instead of what's *really* there?

Most people battle this tendency almost every day, and you've probably noticed it before, especially in group situations. For example, your shuttle from the airport to the hotel has a flat tire, delaying everyone's arrival. Some passengers freak out and complain in a way that makes your delay sound personal and unique to them. Others shrug and find a way to pass the time constructively. A few might even enjoy it by striking up a conversation with the person seated next to them.

It all depends on what they expected based on their past experiences and the neural pathways formed as a result. Remember, a lie believed as truth will affect your life as if it were true. Thoughts can similarly cloud and distort the way you see things if your mental lenses are inaccurate. And we all have our own lenses that color how we see things.

"Cognitive bias" is the term social psychologists use for these personally distorted lenses. It refers to a standardized, consistent pattern of deviating from reality in how we see and process things. If you have a cognitive bias you create a subjective, non-real "reality." That construction of reality, *not* actual reality, will dictate how you respond to and behave in the world.

In addition to influencing how you view daily events and individuals, studies show that cognitive bias can also impact a person's view of God. For instance, your relationship with your earthly father often colors how you perceive your Heavenly Father. If you had a good dad who was involved and full of compassion, it will be easier to view God as relational and caring. If you had a father who was absent or abusive, you are more likely to think of God as distant and disinterested. God is the same no matter who your earthly father was or how he treated you, but your filter affects how clearly you can see your Heavenly Father. Same facts. Different filter.

Another challenge with cognitive bias is that it's easier to see it in others than in ourselves. That's what makes them blind spots—if we knew it was a bias, we wouldn't have it.

Recognizing your own cognitive biases is important, though, if you're going to overcome your negative way of thinking about certain things. Said another way, the way you see things isn't necessarily accurate, which means you're basically hitting replay on your previous experiences rather than living in the present moment.

If you're not engaged in the present moment, then you're likely stuck in the past or the future. The problem then becomes that no matter how hard you try, you cannot control what's happened in the past or what will happen in the future. So you end up feeling powerless or trapped, which sends you right back into old negative neural ruts.

Living in the present, though, offers some good news. While it's true that you cannot control everything that happens to you, here's the silver lining: You *can* control how you perceive it. Rather than react immediately, hit pause and take a deep breath. You realize that despite feeling overwhelmed by emotion in the moment, such as anger or fear, and feeling like you don't have a choice, you actually do have a choice about how you perceive the situation and then act on it.

Social psychologists call this "cognitive reframing." It's when we learn to identify and correct irrational thinking. We could say it's when we un-bias our bias. Reframing is when we decide we're not going to hang on to old perceptions that may have worked against us. We are going to choose a different, more God-accurate, more productive way of thinking.

As you continue to allow God to rewire your brain in order to win the war in your mind, recognizing your biased lenses is essential in order to use a filter of truth based on God's Word.

EXPLORING GOD'S WORD

No one demonstrates a better example of cognitive reframing than the apostle Paul. You'll recall after his dramatic conversion, he had a new mindset about who Jesus is and how to respond to Christ's followers. Because he lived during the height of the Roman Empire, Paul believed the most strategic place to share the gospel so that it had the greatest impact was Rome. So Paul assumed if he could get to Rome and preach Jesus to the leaders there, it could ignite the fuse to explode the good news of Jesus Christ around the world.

After a number of adventures, or perhaps more accurately called misadventures, Paul finally arrived in Rome. Only, he was not there to share Jesus with government officials. Paul landed in Rome as a prisoner. He was locked up under house arrest, chained to a rotating contingent of guards, and forced to await possible execution. Paul's big splash in the largest known city of his time didn't go as planned. He had prayed for an opportunity to preach there, but this was definitely not what he had imagined.

How did Paul respond to such unexpected circumstances? See for yourself:

Now I want you to know, brothers and sisters, that what has happened to me has actually served to advance the gospel. [13] *As a result, it has become clear throughout the whole palace guard and to everyone else that I am in chains for Christ.* [14] *And because of my chains, most of the brothers and sisters have become confident in the Lord and dare all the more to proclaim the gospel without fear. . . .*

[18] *Yes, and I will continue to rejoice,* [19] *for I know that through your prayers and God's provision of the Spirit of Jesus Christ what has happened to me will turn out for my deliverance.* [20] *I eagerly expect and hope that I will in no way be ashamed, but will have sufficient courage so that now as always Christ will be exalted in my body, whether by life or by death.* [21] *For to me, to live is Christ and to die is gain.* [22] *If I am to go on living in the body, this will mean fruitful labor for me. Yet what shall I choose? I do not know!* [23] *I am torn between the two: I desire to depart and be with*

Christ, which is better by far; [24] but it is more necessary for you that I remain in the body. [25] Convinced of this, I know that I will remain, and I will continue with all of you for your progress and joy in the faith, [26] so that through my being with you again your boasting in Christ Jesus will abound on account of me.

– PHILIPPIANS 1:12–14, 18–26

- According to Paul, how did his arrest and imprisonment serve to advance the gospel? What impact did he have there in Rome despite his circumstances?

- How did Paul's arrest and confinement serve to motivate other believers? Why did the way Paul responded to his situation actually inspire them?

- Why does Paul say that he will continue to rejoice? How does he consider his situation— even if he's executed, which was very possible—a kind of win-win?

- What do you suppose Paul means when he wrote that for him "to live is Christ and to die is gain" (verse 21)? What is Paul focused on regardless of whether he lives or dies?

- What does Paul imply he would choose if his destiny was left up to him? Yet why does Paul concede his preference is probably not the most productive choice?

- With the concept of cognitive reframing in mind, how would you say Paul has reframed his situation? Is this just a positive spin or a different way of seeing his circumstances?

REFLECTING ON THE TRUTH

You've likely been where Paul was. Perhaps not literally chained to a guard during house arrest, but you've probably faced situations that went off the rails. You expected events to unfold one way when they suddenly unravel completely. You worked hard to achieve a particular goal only to discover it's not what you thought it was. You prayed for God to give you direction only to find yourself facing obstacles and conflicts left and right.

The fact that life circumstances rarely go as you plan or expect reveals just how little control you actually have over your life. Instead, you're wise to trust God and follow his lead. Which is challenging when nothing in your life makes sense or an unexpected loss leaves you reeling. How can you not sink into despair and give in to hopelessness?

By keeping your faith, of course, but an important tool for remaining strong is reframing. Instead of growing cynical and expecting the worst in those moments, you trust that God knows what he's doing—even if you can't see it or understand what's going on. As you focus on your ability to reframe certain events and circumstances, use the following questions to help you reflect and reevaluate how you view them.

- If you had been in Paul's place when he was arrested and confined in Rome, how would you have responded? Would your letter to other believers be similar or vastly different? Why?

- When you experience unexpected disappointment, a sudden loss, or a devastating turn of events, how do you typically respond in the moment? Are you more prone to shut down emotionally or to explode emotionally?

- Why is it so challenging to reframe events that don't make sense or align with your expectations? What's required in order to reframe them?

- How would you explain the difference between putting a positive spin on a painful situation, such as losing your job, and reframing it by faith?

- When have you recently struggled to understand what God was doing in your life or where he was leading you? How did you respond then? Now?

- When you consider your life's greatest losses and most painful moments, why do you continue to trust in God and his goodness? What do you do with events that seem challenging for you to reframe?

CHANGING YOUR STRATEGY

Expectations often create all kinds of destructive neural pathways. If your expectations are unmet, then you have to face the pain, disappointment, and frustration of not experiencing what you wanted. If your expectations are met, however, then you're left longing for things to remain the way you want them. Either way, your expectations seem to set you up for losing your mental battles.

Granted, the hard moments and tough times are the most challenging. You hate feeling stuck in them and unable to overcome the feelings that haunt you, but you cannot deny the traumatic impact such incidents have had on you and your life. Unfortunately, these formative moments can become the lens through which you view what happens for the rest of your life. They form your cognitive bias, the frame you use to define your reality.

These turning points become the dots you connect in order to tell yourself a story in which you're cast as a loser, a victim, a struggler who can never get ahead. These plot points might pivot on unbelievable betrayal, times of shame and embarrassment, and losses that left empty places in your heart.

While no one can avoid some hard moments along the way, you have a choice about moving through them or taking them with you for the rest of your life. You don't have to get trapped in a freeze-frame moment reliving the trauma of past abuse, the heartache of a family tragedy, or the rage ignited by a social injustice.

If you want to win the war in your mind, then you must thaw out those frozen frames. With God's help, you can rewrite the story you've been telling yourself. You can dare to believe that God, the ultimate Author and Finisher of your faith, knows best even in your worst moments. With this goal in mind, it's time to identify your own cognitive biases and the flawed perspectives—and collateral damage—resulting from them.

What are some of the events with the greatest negative impact on the story you tell yourself about who you are, who God is, and what your life is like? After listing each one, try to pinpoint how these events colored your thinking and created distorted lenses. Provide examples or evidence of the consequences you've experienced because of each cognitive bias you're carrying.

IMPACTFUL EVENT	RESULTING COGNITIVE BIAS	EXAMPLES/EVIDENCE
1.		
2.		
3.		
4.		
5.		

EXERCISING THE EXCHANGE

Using the same events that you just listed, now think about how you can reframe them by considering other, larger perspectives. What are some of the positive outcomes of these events, no matter how painful or devastating they may be? After listing as many blessings as possible emerging from each event, think about how you can reinforce this new way of seeing it from a more heavenly, eternal perspective. For each one, come up with one small action step that will help you reframe that event and its impact on your thinking.

For example, if you were embarrassed as a teenager when giving a book report in front of your class, you may have felt shamed and traumatized to the point that you avoid speaking in front of groups. You see others, especially in group settings as hostile hecklers waiting to mock you and humiliate you, much like your peers did a long time ago.

As you reframe this event, you might realize how fearing and avoiding public speaking has forced you to be more relational in one-on-one situations. While you hate speaking at meetings, you are great at connecting with new neighbors and prospective clients. So, you might list positive outcomes such as relating better with individuals, having more compassion for others, and exercising strong interpersonal communication skills. To reinforce your reframing, you might volunteer to facilitate a small panel discussion at work, lead prayer time for your small group, or mentor the three new hires in your department.

IMPACTFUL EVENT	POSITIVE OUTCOMES	REINFORCING ACTION STEP
1.		
2.		
3.		
4.		
5.		

WHAT GOD DIDN'T DO

Sometimes we need to thank God for what he didn't do.

CRAIG GROESCHEL

Everyone experiences painful events—some obvious and life-changing and others more subtle and personal—that shape our thinking and influence how we see the world. In our suffering we understandably feel confused, angry, and frustrated in our faith. We can't understand why God would allow these terrible events to happen to us or why he wouldn't give us what we've prayed to receive for so long.

Left unchecked, this spiritual bias can cumulatively undermine your faith. So often when you experience loss, frustration, impatience, resentment, doubt, or confusion, you fail to trust that God is up to something for your later good. You lose sight of the fact that God loves you too much to give you everything you ask for or think you want. It's easy to thank God for what he's done for you and to praise him for the many blessings poured into your life, but to win the war for your mind, it's vital that you also learn to thank God for what he didn't do.

Yes, this is not easy to do, nor will it be a one-time shift in your thinking. It requires deliberate focus on seeing your life in ways different than what you've grown accustomed to seeing. But it's more than worth the ongoing effort. Think about some of the things you've wanted and prayers you've prayed. Aren't you so glad God didn't do what you hoped he would?

Think about some of the worst circumstances you've had to go through in your life. You never would have chosen them, maybe you prayed God would pull you out of them, but didn't they help you grow in ways that are crucial to who you are today?

Think about some of the best parts of your life right now. Aren't some of them things you never imagined or planned for, but were just serendipitous shooting stars flung into your life by the Father of the heavenly lights?

It can take a long time to recognize the blessings that come from what he didn't do, but when you have your *aha!* moment, it's more than worth the wait. This practice is a disciplined habit that helps you reframe your past instead of getting stuck in the painful times of disappointment, discouragement, and distress. You realize God's ways are higher than yours, his plans are better than yours, his love for you exceeds giving you everything you ask for. With this perspective, you grow wiser and learn to trust that he is working for you even when you aren't aware of it or able to see the way he's moving on your behalf.

Instead of feeling like a victim of random circumstances in a chaotic world, you see that you have a God who has protected you, often from yourself, in ways you didn't realize.

What happened remains the same, but you reframe with the realization of a new truth.

If you want to win the war for your mind, then you'll want to learn to thank God for what he didn't do.

EXPLORING GOD'S WORD

Look at the life of almost anyone in the Bible, and you can see the way God used them, protected them, and blessed them by what he didn't do. While many of them may not have realized it, there's one man who endured more than a few trials and tribulations yet eventually recognized God's hand at work throughout his ordeals. Joseph certainly had more than a few turning points colored by loss and injustice, including his brothers' jealousy and threat on his life, their abandonment in selling him into slavery, and his false arrest and imprisonment based on the vengeful testimony of Potiphar's wife.

Eventually, however, Joseph's faithfulness was rewarded. Pharaoh removed him from prison in order for Joseph to interpret the leader's troubling dreams that no one else could decipher. Joseph not only accurately told Pharaoh what the dreams meant but demonstrated wisdom in how to make plans and take action in response to their significance. Consequently, Pharaoh made Joseph second-in-command and placed him in charge of preparations for the upcoming years of abundance and famine foretold in his dreams.

Sure enough, as the prophetic dreams became reality, a great famine occurred, but Egypt was prepared thanks to Joseph's trust in God and willingness to serve. When Joseph's brothers then came down from Israel to purchase food, Joseph had the perfect opportunity for payback. While he had some fun scaring them a little (see Genesis 44), Joseph ultimately demonstrated his ability to reframe all that had happened to him as evidenced by his response upon returning home to bury his father.

> [15] When Joseph's brothers saw that their father was dead, they said, "What if Joseph holds a grudge against us and pays us back for all the wrongs we did to him?" [16] So they sent word to Joseph, saying, "Your father left these instructions before he died: [17] 'This is what you are to say to Joseph: I ask you to forgive your brothers the sins and the wrongs they committed in treating you so badly.' Now please forgive the sins of the servants of the God of your father." When their message came to him, Joseph wept.
>
> [18] His brothers then came and threw themselves down before him. "We are your slaves," they said.
>
> [19] But Joseph said to them, "Don't be afraid. Am I in the place of God? [20] You intended to harm me, but God intended it for good to accomplish what is now being done, the saving of many lives. [21] So then, don't be afraid. I will provide for you and your children." And he reassured them and spoke kindly to them.
>
> GENESIS 50:15–21

- How do Joseph's brothers expect him to act toward them upon his arrival home? Why is this a logical, understandable expectation?

- How does the response of Jacob's brothers reinforce how they had treated him all along? Why are they still deceiving him, in this case about their father's instructions prior to his death, in hopes of manipulating him?

- Upon hearing his brothers' fabricated dying declaration from their father and their plea for forgiveness, how does Joseph react? Why do you suppose he reacted this way?

- While his brothers beg mercy because they know Joseph has the upper hand, what is the basis for Joseph's merciful response? What does Joseph consider as the source of his power?

- Based on his response to his brothers (see verse 20), how has Joseph reframed his brothers' jealousy, betrayal, abandonment, and deception? What allows Joseph to see God at work even in the midst of his brothers' intention to harm him?

- What actions does Joseph take to support his words of forgiveness and mercy? How does he treat his brothers based on his ability to reframe the suffering in his life and see God at work?

REFLECTING ON THE TRUTH

When others intend to harm you, it's tough to be as gracious and merciful as Joseph. In fact, it only occurs when you're relying on God's presence, power, and purpose in your life. Otherwise, your view is limited to what you've seen and experienced. Even when silver linings emerge, some people become so fixated on their sufferings that they refuse to acknowledge God's higher purpose for past events.

Joseph told his brothers that despite their intentions to harm him—in fact, to kill him—God was actively at work in the events of his life. Each moment of pain, each act of betrayal, each second of suffering was not in vain. While the plot points of Joseph's story seem like a roller coaster ride of ups and downs, Joseph learned to experience the ride in the security of his faith in God. As a result, Joseph provides a powerful model for how we can learn to reflect on our lives and reframe even the most unimaginable moments.

- If you were in Joseph's place when his brothers came to Egypt to purchase food, how would you have responded? Why?

- When have you had opportunities for revenge or payback on those who have caused you harm or intended to hurt you? How have you handled such opportunities?

- Who are the people in your life that have been the hardest for you to forgive? Why is forgiving them an important part of reframing past events by trusting God was at work in your suffering?

- Why is it difficult to let go of the pain caused by past events in your life? How does clinging to the pain from your toughest times create a distorted lens?

- When have you stepped out in faith by acting with kindness and generosity despite your suffering? What impact did your actions have on those around you?

- What must you surrender in order to trust God's goodness at work even in your darkest times? How does this kind of faith help you reframe the story of your life?

CHANGING YOUR STRATEGY

In order to reframe past painful events and thank God for what he didn't do, you will want to face moments and memories you might rather avoid. Times when you got what you wanted only to realize it wasn't really what you wanted. Moments when you felt like you had the rug of security pulled out from under you. Events that unfolded in ways directly opposite those you expected. Words said by others that pierced your heart with rejection, betrayal, injustice, and condemnation.

Like venturing into the basement of your mind, you may find it overwhelming to know where to start sorting and reframing past events. If this is the case, start with what's manageable. Choose one and invite God to give you courage, wisdom, strength, and discernment. Ask for his help as you seek to see your life through his perspective. Instead of asking *why* something happened, ask *how* you can see it differently and move forward.

Changing your strategy in order to reframe past events requires some honest conversations between you and the Lord. He knows, of course, what's in your heart, but you may be in denial or refusing to surrender old baggage because you've grown so accustomed to its weight on your back. Considering what God didn't do in your past also presents an opportunity for you to be honest about any lingering anger, doubt, and resistance keeping you distant in your faith. Confess to God anything holding you back as you surrender your old lenses for his eternal perspective. Here's a prayer to get you started, but ask God's Spirit to guide you as you make it your own.

Heavenly Father, it's so hard to see my past losses and painful crossroads from your perspective, but I'm willing to try. I surrender my anger, my ego, my pride, my control, and my entitled attitude. Help me to see clearly without the distortion of old fears and tired defenses. I want to trust you, Lord, with all of my being. I want to believe, just as Joseph believed, that what others intend for my harm, you intend for my good and for the advancement of your kingdom. Amen.

EXERCISING THE EXCHANGE

Review chapter 8 in *Winning the War in Your Mind,* including the exercise "Unanswered Prayers." Looking back on your life, continue adding to this list of blessings you see as the result of God not giving you what you thought you wanted at the time. Try not only to glimpse why you're grateful God didn't answer your prayers then but trace the resulting positive outcomes right up to where you are right now. After you've come up with several unanswered prayers, spend some time thinking about your current prayer requests. Are there any you want to revise based on your motive for asking?

COLLATERAL GOODNESS

When we reframe what happened in our yesterdays, that changes our todays. We are able to experience life without the old, negative cognitive bias and start seeing through the lens of God's goodness.

CRAIG GROESCHEL

Imagine you're on a flight to an exotic, tropical vacation destination, say, Hawaii. You've been planning and saving up for months and months. Reading online reviews of hotels and restaurants, beaches and gardens, hiking trails and evening luaus. But when you get off the plane, you're not where you thought you'd be—you're in Alaska.

Instead of ocean breezes, you're shivering from the Arctic wind slicing through your beachwear-clad body. Not only are you furious upon arrival, but you discover you will spend your entire vacation in snow-covered lodges instead of open-air cabanas. Obviously, you're disappointed, angry, and dismayed by the change in venue, but you also have a choice about what you do now that you're in Alaska. Because Alaska is an awesome place, filled with natural beauty and amazing wildlife.

Simply put, you have a choice: you can embrace being in Alaska and make the most of your time there. Or you can complain, rage, worry, yell, and be miserable while you're there by focusing on what you've lost and what you're missing out on. You can hate Alaska because it's not Hawaii, or you can enjoy being there because that's where you are.

It's not only vacation destinations that provide you with opportunities to choose. Basically, you will always find what you are looking for no matter where you are. If you expect to be unhappy, you will be unhappy no matter how things are going. If you expect to be happy, then you'll experience happiness despite whatever limitations or challenges circumstances might impose.

When you reframe what happened in your yesterdays, it changes your todays. You are able to experience life without the old, negative cognitive bias and start seeing through the lens of God's goodness. In other words, reframing allows you to pre-frame.

Pre-framing is choosing how you will view something *before* it happens. Instead of getting there and letting your old frame take over, leading you to interpret what might actually be positive as negative, you proactively choose the frame you will use to evaluate your experience. Just as reframing taught you how to recognize and appreciate what God didn't do, pre-framing helps you anticipate the positive ways God is at work in your life right now and into your future. Instead of worrying about the collateral damage the next unexpected event or crisis causes, you look for God's collateral goodness.

Like most thought habits, collateral goodness requires practice. If you look for what's bad, you will find bad. If you look for what's negative, you will find plenty to be negative about. If you look for things to be critical about, there is always going to be something to criticize.

But if you look for God's goodness, you will also see it. You'll start recognizing God's fingerprints in situations and may occasionally even feel like he's offering you little gifts throughout your day. As you pay attention to how God is working, you will find yourself seeing good in people. It will change your relationships. Your attitude will be transformed. And the right attitude always precedes the right actions.

Winning the war in your mind requires trusting God to know what's best for you, even when it's different from what you want, need, or think you desire. It means expecting to find collateral goodness as you follow his guidance into your joyful future. Even when you're in Alaska instead of Hawaii.

EXPLORING GOD'S WORD

Perhaps traveling forces us to deal with our expectations in ways that other events cannot. Moving from one home to another, especially when it's in a different country and culture, is naturally stressful. But how we view those journeys largely depends on what we expect. That's certainly the case for one woman in the Bible who felt like God had abandoned her due to the tragic losses in her life.

Faced with a famine in their homeland, Naomi accompanied her husband, Elimelek, and their two sons to Moab. After Elimelek died there, Naomi's sons married Moabite women. Then after ten years, the unthinkable happened and both of Naomi's sons died. Suddenly, she was a widow with no adult sons to provide for her. Alone in a foreign culture, Naomi only had her two daughters-in-law by her side.

They heard that the famine had ended back in Judah, so the three women set out to travel back to Naomi's hometown, Bethlehem. Along the way, Naomi couldn't shake her lens of grief, despair, and loneliness and urged the two younger women to turn back to Moab:

> [11] *But Naomi said, "Return home, my daughters. Why would you come with me? Am I going to have any more sons, who could become your husbands?* [12] *Return home, my daughters; I am too old to have another husband. Even if I thought there was still hope for me—even if I had a husband tonight and then gave birth to sons—* [13] *would you wait until they grew up? Would you remain unmarried for them? No, my daughters. It is more bitter for me than for you, because the* LORD*'s hand has turned against me!"*
>
> – RUTH 1:11–13

While Orpah heeded her mother-in-law's advice, Naomi's other daughter-in-law, Ruth, refused to leave her side. She made it clear that no matter how much worse their circumstances might become, she was committed to Naomi. Realizing it was pointless to argue with Ruth, they continued on their journey until their reached Bethlehem, where no one recognized the distraught, grief-weary woman they once knew as Naomi.

²² "Don't call me Naomi," she told them. "Call me Mara, because the Almighty has made my life very bitter. ²¹ I went away full, but the LORD has brought me back empty. Why call me Naomi? The LORD has afflicted me; the Almighty has brought misfortune upon me."

²² So Naomi returned from Moab accompanied by Ruth the Moabite, her daughter-in-law, arriving in Bethlehem as the barley harvest was beginning.

– RUTH 1:20–22

As they settled in Bethlehem, Ruth's attitude and expectations were remarkably different than Naomi's. Instead of expecting the worst because of all the hard things that had happened, Ruth trusted that God will take care of them, provide for them, and bless them with his goodness. If you know the rest of the story, then you know the kind of happy ending Ruth experienced when she married Boaz, a distant relative of her deceased husband, with whom she had a son. Despite her previous pessimistic perspective, new grandma Naomi realized that God had not abandoned her after all.

¹⁴ The women said to Naomi: "Praise be to the LORD, who this day has not left you without a guardian-redeemer. May he become famous throughout Israel! ¹⁵ He will renew your life and sustain you in your old age. For your daughter-in-law, who loves you and who is better to you than seven sons, has given him birth."

¹⁶ Then Naomi took the child in her arms and cared for him. ¹⁷ The women living there said, "Naomi has a son!" And they named him Obed. He was the father of Jesse, the father of David.

– RUTH 4:14–17

- Why did Naomi urge her two daughters-in-law to return to their homeland of Moab after they had started on their journey with her to Bethlehem? What reasons does Naomi cite as the basis for her conclusion?

- How does Naomi's desire to change her name reflect her distorted lens? How did her bitterness color her circumstances even after Ruth remained with her and accompanied her to Bethlehem?

- How do the people in Naomi's community there in Bethlehem serve as barometers of her attitude? How do they also serve as a kind of reality check for her?

- How was Ruth better to Naomi than seven sons would have been? How did Ruth's love and commitment to her change the way Naomi saw her life's story?

- What's the significance of including the name of Naomi's grandson and the generations after him? How does this reflect the way Naomi's story was reframed?

- Looking back at her life, what are the things that Naomi could have thanked God for not doing?

REFLECTING ON THE TRUTH

In the midst of a health battle, financial crisis, loss of a loved one, or a devastating betrayal, pain can blind you from seeing beyond your own suffering. When the pain is so intense, it's understandable that you can't see other perspectives at first. You want to trust God and walk by faith, but when you're suddenly pushed to the ground and your world goes dark, it's hard to find your footing.

But in order to get up again, you can choose to believe that God is there with you and will not abandon you. You can take that first step, no matter how shaky, and then another and the next. Naomi's life was turned upside down when the men she loved most were taken from her. She couldn't imagine ever being secure and happy again and assumed God had given up on her.

Perhaps you have experienced similar losses that led to a crisis of faith. You might even be going through one now. Wherever you are on your journey of faith, though, don't give up. And don't give in to the negative, cynical, skeptical whispers of the enemy. He loves to heap on when you're down and out.

Instead, dare to reframe your losses until you can pre-frame what's ahead of you.

- When have you felt like Naomi in the midst of a season of loss or a crisis of faith? How did you respond?

- Who has stood by you during your trials the way Ruth stayed with Naomi? How did the loving concern of others reveal God's presence despite your overwhelming emotions?

- How have you seen God work following a hard time or challenging season? How did he redeem your losses and use your experiences for his purposes?

- If you were to change your name, like Naomi wanting to be known as Mara or Bitter, what would you change it to, based on your hardest battles? If you were to change it based on trusting God is at work, what would you want to be called?

- Based on where you are right now in your journey of faith, what's required for you to grow closer to God? How is he the source of your future hope?

- What's your greatest barrier or personal obstacle to trusting God with your future happiness?

CHANGING YOUR STRATEGY

God's timing rarely aligns with our own, but as the old saying goes, "he's always on time." Just as children have to learn the benefits of delayed gratification, we're wise to accept that we can't necessarily have what we want when we want it—and this is a good thing. Because our human limitations and cognitive biases don't give us the big picture, the eternal perspective that God has on the entire epic story of our lives.

As you continue to practice the principle of reframing, you learn to let go of your earthly schedule and instead live by God's divine daily planner. We're told, "Many are the plans in a person's heart, but it is the LORD's purpose that prevails" (Proverbs 19:21). While we're called to plan ahead, work hard toward goals, and use our time wisely, we must remember that God knows best. We live in the tension between being good stewards of each day and surrendering our agendas in order to receive what God calls us to do.

With this goal in mind, spend some of your valuable time considering how you can be more open-handed with your future plans while expecting to experience God's collateral goodness along the way. Use these questions to get you started thinking about what it looks like to trust the Lord with every second of every day.

- Do you think of yourself as more of a visionary planner who always prepares for what's ahead or a flexible flyer who remains untethered and spontaneous? How has being this way influenced your expectations as you move ahead?

- When have you expected the worst and experienced it? How much of what you experienced was due to your negative expectations?

- When has a big disappointment turned into a surprising discovery or enjoyable experience? How did you make the shift from your disappointment to your discovery?

- Looking back, when have you seen God's timing work out in ways far better than your own? How can you trust that he's always working in your life at a divine pace?

- Rather than lowering your expectations in order to pre-frame future events, what would happen if you expected more from God? What prevents you from hoping for more from him?

- How would you describe the current rhythm and pace of God's guidance in your life? Are you waiting on him to reveal your next step—or is he waiting on you to step out in faith?

EXERCISING THE EXCHANGE

With God's help, you can decide the lens that you will look through moving forward. In order to experience all that God has for you and wants to bless you with, it's time to expect to see more of his collateral goodness. It's always there, but when you begin paying attention and noticing it, you will be surprised what a difference it can make in how you think, feel, and act.

Looking ahead, it's time to create a new vision for yourself and your life. Where do you see yourself one year from now? Remember, the direction of your thoughts today will determine where they take you tomorrow. Spend a few minutes in prayer and then write a description of who you want to be twelve months from now.

Regardless of your present circumstances, do your best to pre-frame your future. What situations do you know you will be walking into? What would be the most positive, life-building, God-honoring, mutually edifying way for you to approach that moment? Fill in the blanks below to get you started as you pre-frame your next steps.

One year from now I see myself thinking more about _____ and less about _____.

One year from now I will spend more time _____ rather than _____.

One year from now I will be closer to God because _____.

One year from now I will be winning the war for my mind because _____ _____.

PART 4

THE REJOICE PRINCIPLE

REVIVE YOUR SOUL, RECLAIM YOUR LIFE

Putting everything together and practicing all you've learned, you will be equipped to identify your mental triggers and overcome them through the power of prayer. Old thought patterns no longer have the same power over you as you redirect mental ruts to focus on God's truth. You recognize the power that praising God and giving him thanks can have to change your attitude, your thoughts, and your behavior. As your soul experiences revival, you celebrate because you know that your life will never be the same. Relying on the power of God and claiming the victory Jesus secured for you on the cross, you have won the battle in your mind!

As you practice the Rejoice Principle, you will:

- Cultivate your awareness of God's presence even when you feel anxious, stressed, and upset.
- Develop strategies for relying on God's help and living by faith when life overwhelms you.
- Rely on the perspective of praising God to change the way you think about events, relationships, and problems.
- Give thanks and praise to God for his blessings, large and small, on a daily basis.
- Learn to look through hard times and moments when you stumble, rather than allowing them to preoccupy your thoughts and block your momentum.
- Commit to winning the war for your mind as you grow stronger in your faith and closer to God each day.

PROBLEMS, PANIC,
AND PRESENCE

When you've had enough, God is enough.

CRAIG GROESCHEL

By now you've learned that your life will always move in the direction of your strongest thoughts. But sometimes it seems like a huge wave of negative thoughts comes crashing down on you before you even realized the tide was coming in. Something triggered a panic button inside you, and now your entire body is on red alert. You feel tense, anxious, and braced for action. You're worried, afraid, and hyper-aware of your surroundings. Adrenaline courses through you to fuel your instinctive decision toward flight, fight, or freeze.

This response results from a little almond shaped part of your brain called the amygdala, which is largely responsible for primal emotions and survival instincts.

When you're afraid, the amygdala goes into action like a battleship preparing to strike. It causes that spike of adrenaline that prepares your body to defend itself, run away, or freeze in place until the danger passes.

That's a good thing if you're walking in the park and suddenly a ferocious, growling, snarling dog springs at you from the woods. Your body reacts immediately to either protect yourself from Killer's frothing jaws or to outrun him to safety. You know now is not the time to practice your skills as a dog-whisperer.

The amygdala, however, cannot always discern what's really a danger and what's related to past experience that caused you to react with strong emotions. The way it responds to a noise in the middle of the night letting you know someone is breaking in your house is the way it responds to a ping from your phone revealing an overdraft alert on your bank account. In either case, you're immediately on edge and know you need to respond.

Only, what if you can't take action or the alert turns out to be a false alarm? Maybe you can't fix the overdraft in your account until tomorrow or maybe it's a tech glitch with your bank's new software.

In certain situations, you may feel like your amygdala is out of whack. It alerts you to danger, but you can't identify the trigger. Suddenly, your response is not as clear cut as fight or flight. Sometimes you panic and don't know how to push through it or what to do about it. It's like your body is reacting to something dangerous at the same time your mind is trying to figure out what's going on. You know you're panicked and freaking out, but you can't find your way out.

When these moments occur, another part of your brain, the prefrontal cortex, kicks in to help your slightly confused amygdala know if the threat is real. The prefrontal cortex is the logical part of the brain, which God gave you to keep the emotional part of your brain in check. The prefrontal cortex tries to remind you that not all dogs off leash are rabid beasts about to attack and that all sounds in the night are not necessarily someone breaking in.

Despite the help of your prefrontal cortex, you can still struggle to regulate your amygdala and avoid overreactions. The best way to balance and regulate your internal alarm system is to insulate it with God's peace. His peace is the negotiator who can settle the rest of your body into a calm, tranquil state of trusting God, no matter what threat you face, real or perceived.

If you want to win the war for your mind, you'll want to experience God's presence and peace in the midst of your problems and panic.

EXPLORING GOD'S WORD

When you feel as though you're at your breaking point, it's hard to trust God has a plan. And it may be even harder to pray, praise, and worship God in the midst of your avalanche of angst. But that's when you can choose to act in faith in order to win the intense battle raging in your mind. That's when you must seek shelter in the arms of the Almighty and trust that he's got you. That no matter what you're facing, he will see you through it.

It may also help to know that you're not alone, that everyone feels this way at times, that even God's chosen prophets can get to a point where they've had enough and want to give up. That was the case with Elijah, a prophet God chose to confront Israel's evil King Ahab and his wicked wife, Jezebel. Infuriated by Elijah's bold confidence in God, King Ahab threatened to kill Elijah, but the prophet managed to elude his hunter and orchestrated a spiritual showdown between Ahab's idols, and the 850 false priests serving them, and the Living God, represented solely by Elijah.

Elijah proved his point in dramatic fashion, humiliating Ahab and Jezebel and spotlighting the power and glory of God. Rather than put the matter to rest, this victory only made matters worse. Jezebel threatened to kill Elijah and got into his head. Suddenly, the prophet's entire world seemed to crumble, and he had reached his breaking point.

> [3] *Elijah was afraid and ran for his life. When he came to Beersheba in Judah, he left his servant there,* [4] *while he himself went a day's journey into the wilderness. He came to a broom bush, sat down under it and prayed that he might die. "I have had enough, LORD," he said. "Take my life; I am no better than my ancestors."* [5] *Then he lay down under the bush and fell asleep.*
>
> *All at once an angel touched him and said, "Get up and eat."* [6] *He looked around, and there by his head was some bread baked over hot coals, and a jar of water. He ate and drank and then lay down again.*
>
> [7] *The angel of the LORD came back a second time and touched him and said, "Get up and eat, for the journey is too much for you."* [8] *So he got up and ate and drank. Strengthened by that food, he traveled forty days and forty nights until he reached Horeb, the mountain of God.* [9] *There he went into a cave and spent the night.*
>
> *And the word of the LORD came to him: "What are you doing here, Elijah?"*

¹⁰ He replied, "I have been very zealous for the LORD God Almighty. The Isra-elites have rejected your covenant, torn down your altars, and put your prophets to death with the sword. I am the only one left, and now they are trying to kill me too."

¹¹ The LORD said, "Go out and stand on the mountain in the presence of the LORD, for the LORD is about to pass by."

Then a great and powerful wind tore the mountains apart and shattered the rocks before the LORD, but the LORD was not in the wind. After the wind there was an earthquake, but the LORD was not in the earthquake. ¹² After the earthquake came a fire, but the LORD was not in the fire. And after the fire came a gentle whis-per. ¹³ When Elijah heard it, he pulled his cloak over his face and went out and stood at the mouth of the cave.

— 1 KINGS 19:3–13

- Knowing God had just empowered Elijah to defeat Ahab's idols, why do you suppose Elijah was suddenly afraid and ran for his life? Why did he lose his confidence in God's ability to protect him from Ahab and Jezebel?

- Why did Elijah leave his servant behind before running into the wilderness? Why do you think he wanted to be alone?

- What do you think Elijah meant when he told God, "I am no better than my ancestors"? How did this belief relate to his despair and desire to have his life ended?

- Why did the angel sent by God instruct Elijah to eat and drink and allow him to sleep another night? What does this tell us about the condition of Elijah's physical as well as mental health?

- How would you paraphrase Elijah's response to God about why the prophet was there? After all, didn't God direct Elijah to travel to this destination?

- After such a dramatic display of natural phenomenon, why does God whisper to get Elijah's attention? Why do you think it's God's whisper that prompts Elijah to get up and prepare to leave his cave?

REFLECTING ON THE TRUTH

You may not have evil kings and queens threatening your life, but you probably can relate to Elijah's experience, nonetheless. Your toughest times may even have occurred right after some of your greatest accomplishments or spiritual highs. One minute you're celebrating God's goodness and enjoying his blessings and the next you're overwhelmed by life's demands and don't want to get out of bed.

During these times when you feel like running away from life, you will probably struggle to rein in your thoughts and focus on what's true. When emotions overflow and your amygdala keeps lighting up like a carnival game, you may not be able to focus the way you want, let alone focus on what you know is actually true. Despite how painful and draining these times can be, they also present opportunities for intimacy with God. Just as he took care of Elijah and called him out of his cave of despair, God will meet you where you are and meet your needs as well.

- When have you experienced moments similar to Elijah's in proclaiming that you've had enough? What led up to them?

- On a scale of 1 to 10, with 1 being "slightly uncomfortable" and 10 being "debilitating despair," what would you rate your current level of stress? What's contributing to it?

- Like Elijah, have you realized that your physical health often requires attention during these dire times? How has lack of rest, poor sleep habits, unhealthy diet, and dehydration contributed to your major meltdowns?

- When you reach your breaking point, how does your stress and panic usually manifest in your behavior? Do you tend to shut down and go numb or do you tilt toward uncontrollable emotions and overreactions?

- While you may not have literally run away from problems that felt overwhelming, what are some ways you have nonetheless tried to escape or find relief? What behaviors and substances have an addictive appeal during your toughest times?

- When has God whispered to you during a bout with stress, anxiety, panic, and/or depression? How did recognizing his presence in the midst of your storm help you find your way out?

CHANGING YOUR STRATEGY

When you're at the end of your rope, remember that God's truth still has the power to set you free. Sometimes this means realizing that you can let go of the rope you're holding that used to seem so vitally important. The old adage to "let go and let God" proves true when you recognize the false beliefs and biased conditional thinking that only compound the difficult circumstances you're facing.

Other times, experiencing the power of God's truth during intensely stressful times means discovering his presence and peace even if your circumstances don't change. You realize that your experience plus God's presence is enough.

This is the secret that Elijah learned. The experience he already had—with God providing miraculously for him, sustaining him through the worst of times—plus God's presence, was enough. He could come out of his cave, trust God to lead and guide him, and discover a renewed sense of purpose to continue serving the Lord and enjoying his life.

The same is true for you. You may be feeling burdened, overwhelmed, and anxious by the load you're carrying. Maybe your soul feels crushed by the weight of burdens bearing down on you. Their weight causes you to panic at times, to want to give up, to do something drastic like running away and living in a cave.

But in those moments, just remember: When you've had enough, God is enough. To jog your memory and refocus your attention, practice what you've learned so far. You need a declaration of peace, patience, perseverance, and power. Ground yourself in God's Word and his promises to you as his beloved child. With this in mind, draft a short psalm based on favorite verses, passages used in your previous declarations, and what you know to be true of God's presence in your life. Filling in the blanks below will get you started.

MY PSALM OF GOD'S PRESENCE AND PEACE

God is with me even when I feel _____.

My worries about _____ and my fears about

_____ are not more powerful than the Lord.

The promise from God's Word I will cling to during times of stress and panic is this:

_____.

Knowing how much God loves me and how close he is to me right now, I can focus

on _____ rather than

_____.

EXERCISING THE EXCHANGE

When you're overwhelmed and don't know how to go on, the most essential thing is for your mind to focus on the presence of God rather than the absence of whatever you think would solve your problems. God alone is bigger than your problems and more powerful than any force on earth. You are never alone because he is with you and he is enough for you. His strength sustains you. He watches over you and he guides you with his loving eye upon you. If you listen, you will hear his whisper drawing you closer.

As you plan ahead for times when your amygdala may go into overdrive without an immediate tangible threat, think about the tactics you can employ to experience God's presence in the midst of your panic. Here are a few that might be helpful, but the greatest benefit will come from the ones you make uniquely your own. Add to this list and choose one to practice regularly at least once a day for the next week.

- Stop what I'm doing and read my "Psalm of God's Presence and Peace" that I wrote in the previous exercise. Then read it again—out loud.
- Find a quiet place where I won't be interrupted or disturbed and spend five minutes in prayer, pouring out my concerns to God.
- Call or text a close friend and ask them to pray for me right then.
- Go back and reread chapter 10, especially the section titled, "Experiencing God's Presence," in *Winning the War for Your Mind*.
- Focus on a past situation when God saw me through a difficult dilemma or painful problem.

THE PERSPECTIVE OF PRAISE

If it's big enough to worry about, then it's big enough to pray about.

CRAIG GROESCHEL

Focusing on God's presence changes how you view your circumstances. It changes how you think about them, the decisions you make, and the actions you take. And there's a simple reason for why being mindful of his presence is so vitally important: If you forget God is there with you, then you're not going to talk to him.

When you don't focus on God's presence, you don't pray. Instead, you go it alone. You get swept up in the current of your strongest thoughts and most overwhelming emotions. You find your actions following behind the wave of negative, destructive thoughts. You begin losing the war for your mind and losing sight of God's collateral goodness that's all around you.

When you realize God is with you, however, you inevitably want to talk to him. You want his help. You want to lean on his peace and connect to his power. When you realize you can talk to God, then instead of just going with the mud-slide of bad thoughts, you can you look up. Looking up, you know you can take shelter in him. Looking up, you find a God who loves you and has the power to help you. Focusing on God's presence habitually reminds you that you're not alone and have Someone to talk to.

This is not just an obvious observation. Remember Paul's instruction for how to deal with panic-inducing circumstances? "Do not be anxious about anything, but in every situation, by prayer and petition, with thanksgiving, present your requests to God" (Philippians 4:6). Notice Paul says "anything" here, which means if it's enough for you to worry about, then it's enough for you to pray about. If it's on your mind, it's on God's heart.

No matter how your thoughts are crashing around in your mind, the best thing you can do to escape their undertow is to pray. Any time you're worried or leaping to worst-case scenarios, any time you're tempted to run away and ignore your problems, any time you're paranoid because things are going so well that you know something bad is bound to happen, the remedy is simply to pray.

If you're intimidated by prayer, then remember that Jesus said you can call God "Abba" when you pray. Abba was the most simple, endearing way to refer to a father back then. Today's equivalent might be daddy, or papa. God is a relational God who loves you and wants to have an intimate relationship with you. So, when you talk to him, you don't have to worry about doing it the right way.

When you're talking to God, when you're aware of his presence as your loving Father, then you can also praise him. Because you'll recall Paul also told us, again in that same letter to the believers in Philippi, "Rejoice in the Lord always. I will say it again: Rejoice!" (Philippians 4:4). Praising the Lord regardless of what's going on or how you feel forces you to shift perspective. And if you're going to win the war in your mind, then a perspective of praise makes all the difference.

EXPLORING GOD'S WORD

Paul isn't the only one who discovered the power of prayer and praise to shift his perspective. Of the many examples in Scripture, one of Jesus' disciples demonstrates the kind of before-and-after change that continues to inspire count-less believers: Simon Peter. A fisherman by trade, Peter emerges in the New Testament as a rough-and-tumble, somewhat impetuous, tell-it-like-it-is kind of guy.

In one of his most famous incidents, Peter drew his sword and cut off the ear of the high priest's servant who had accompanied the authorities arresting Jesus in the Garden of Gethsemane (John 18:10). This reckless act of devoted protection was undermined, however, by Peter's denial of his Master only hours later:

> [54] *Then seizing him [Jesus], they led him away and took him into the house of the high priest. Peter followed at a distance.* [55] *And when some there had kindled a fire in the middle of the courtyard and had sat down together, Peter sat down with them.* [56] *A servant girl saw him seated there in the firelight. She looked closely at him and said, "This man was with him."*
>
> [57] *But he denied it. "Woman, I don't know him," he said.*
>
> [58] *A little later someone else saw him and said, "You also are one of them."*
>
> *"Man, I am not!" Peter replied.*
>
> [59] *About an hour later another asserted, "Certainly this fellow was with him, for he is a Galilean."*
>
> [60] *Peter replied, "Man, I don't know what you're talking about!" Just as he was speaking, the rooster crowed.* [61] *The Lord turned and looked straight at Peter. Then Peter remembered the word the Lord had spoken to him: "Before the rooster crows today, you will disown me three times."* [62] *And he went outside and wept bitterly.*
>
> – LUKE 22:54–62

• What motivated Peter to deny even knowing Jesus after proclaiming his devotion at the Passover supper the night before? In addition to fear for his safety, what other thoughts and emotions were likely running through Peter's mind?

- What are the consequences of Peter's denial of knowing Jesus? What impact does denying him three times have?

- How could Peter have been told by Jesus that he would disown his Master three times before the rooster crowed and yet still do it? What does this quick shift, and Jesus' awareness of it in his follower, reveal about Peter's personality and character?

Peter did not dwell on his failure because his joy upon discovering Christ's resurrection is exuberant. When Peter and some of the other disciples were out fishing, they saw someone on the beach whom Peter immediately recognized as his risen Master. Peter was so excited that he jumped out of the boat and swam to shore, eager to enjoy the breakfast Jesus was preparing for them over an open fire. Afterward, Jesus spoke to Peter and made it clear that his love for this disciple had never changed (all of this is described in John 21).

As further evidence of Peter's ability to move beyond his past mistakes, his ministry after Christ's ascension speaks for itself. His maturity and wisdom emerge clearly when Peter later shares the secret to his transformation:

> [6] *Humble yourselves, therefore, under God's mighty hand, that he may lift you up in due time.* [7] *Cast all your anxiety on him because he cares for you.*
>
> [8] *Be alert and of sober mind. Your enemy the devil prowls around like a roaring lion looking for someone to devour.* [9] *Resist him, standing firm in the faith, because you know that the family of believers throughout the world is undergoing the same kind of sufferings.*
>
> [10] *And the God of all grace, who called you to his eternal glory in Christ, after you have suffered a little while, will himself restore you and make you strong, firm and steadfast.* [11] *To him be the power for ever and ever. Amen.*
>
> — 1 PETER 5:6–11

- Why do you suppose Peter emphasizes the importance of humility in order to experience God's presence? How did Peter's past experiences reinforce this in his own life?

- What advice does Peter impart here about suffering? How does he describe suffering and its benefits?

- Why does Peter shift from urging us to focus on God ("Cast all your anxiety on him because he cares for you") to warning us about the devil's attacks ("Your enemy the devil prowls . . .resist him . . .")? How are the two related?

REFLECTING ON THE TRUTH

Peter tells us that God is inviting us to go to him: "Humble yourselves, therefore, under God's mighty hand, that he may lift you up in due time. Cast all your anxiety on him because he cares for you" (1 Peter 5:6-7). These words resonate even more powerfully when we remember another particular incident in which God's hand literally lifted Peter up when he fell (Matthew 14:22–33). With the other disciples on a boat sailing the Sea of Galilee, Peter had the audacity to believe he could walk on water to Jesus. Then the storm kicked up and Peter's confidence sunk, just as he did when focused on the crashing waves and howling wind. The urgency of his problem caused him to ignore the presence of Jesus.

But then Peter reached out and grabbed the hand of Jesus. His Master lifted him up and saved him from drowning in the choppy, storm-tossed sea. Years later, Peter likely remembered this incident when he encouraged those reading his letter, "Humble yourselves, therefore, under God's mighty hand, that he may lift you up." God is willing to rescue you the same way, when you shift your perspective from panic in the face of problems to his presence and power.

- Can you relate to Peter's struggles to focus on God's presence? When have you denied knowing Christ by choosing to focus on your fears instead?

- How did Peter change in the years between his denial of Jesus prior to the crucifixion and when he wrote this letter encouraging other believers?

- When have you experiencing a stumble or dip in your faith recently? How did you handle the situation to get back on your feet?

- When has the urgency of your problems caused you to panic rather than to reach for the presence of God? How can you experience God's presence the next time you feel overwhelmed or have a panic attack due to life's problems?

- How has God made his presence known to you when you've been caught in one of life's storms? How did you respond to his presence then?

- What does it look like for you to cast all your anxiety on God? Why does Peter seem to see this as evidence of your trust in God's care for you?

CHANGING YOUR STRATEGY

Prayer and praise are essential to change your thinking and to win the war for your mind. The Bible boils down your strategy quite clearly: "Rejoice always, pray without ceasing, give thanks in all circumstances; for this is the will of God in Christ Jesus for you (1 Thessalonians 5:16–18 ESV). In order to become someone who prays all the time, who can choose to rejoice and praise God regardless of circumstances, you may want to change the way you view prayer.

One way to change your perspective on prayer and praise is to evaluate how you usually see them now and to understand the basis for this perspective. If you were called upon to pray aloud in church and became flustered and at a loss for words, then you may occasionally still feel the sting of shame when you pray. If you have a formal, more liturgical church background, you may view prayer as a formal ceremony requiring proper poetic language.

But God just wants you to talk to him, to open your heart to him, and to seek his presence no matter what you're facing. Toward this goal, use the following questions to learn more about your views on prayer and how you can integrate it more fully into daily life.

- How would you describe the way you have learned to pray? What messages and assumptions about prayer did you pick up as a child?

- How often would you say you prayed prior to reading *Winning the War for Your Mind* and completing this workbook? How has your view of prayer changed now?

- What negative associations or bad memories related to prayer do you need to release in order to talk more intimately with God?

- What does it mean for you to "pray without ceasing" considering your present season of life and daily schedule? How can prayer become a natural part of every day?

- When you think about rejoicing always and giving thanks in all circumstances, what obstacles or barriers come to mind? What's required for you to be more grateful and more gracious?

● Knowing what you know now about how to win the war for your mind, how has your prayer life changed? How would you like it to change still?

EXERCISING THE EXCHANGE

Prayer is making the decision to turn to and surrender your feelings and control of your life to God, trusting his promises and power. Paul writes, "Those who are dominated by the sinful nature think about sinful things, but those who are controlled by the Holy Spirit think about things that please the Spirit. So letting your sinful nature control your mind leads to death. But letting the Spirit control your mind leads to life and peace" (Romans 8:5-6 NLT).

If you let your natural, human nature take over, you will be led by runaway, negative thoughts that spiral out of control and lead you in the wrong direction. If you let the Spirit take over, you will be led to life and peace. It's a choice that leads to a practice that leads to a habit that leads to simply being part of you.

To reinforce this practice, review the section, "The God Box," in chapter 11 of *Winning the War in Your Mind*. If you haven't created your God Box already and completed this exercise, then start there. If you know you want to use your God Box a tactic to help you focus your thoughts in a positive way, then feel free to get creative, fancy, or crafty. You can have a God Jar or God Fishbowl or whatever kind of God Container you will actually use the most.

Once your God Box is in place, then it's time to actually use it. Commit to writing a list of at least three worries, concerns, burdens, temptations, mistakes, or regrets you have each day for one full week. Pick a regular time, either morning or evening might work best, and make your thought list to deposit in your God Box. Let God know you're handing these thoughts over to him and trusting him to handle them so that they're no longer weighing on your mind.

At the end of your week, empty your God Box in the trash without rereading what you wrote. Let those thoughts go. You can even burn them if you have a safe permissible place to do so. The key is simply to take those thoughts captive and allow God to have them.

LOOK THROUGH, NOT AT

A change of perspective leads us to praise God.
And praising God changes our perspective.

CRAIG GROESCHEL

Y ou will never accidentally change the way you think.

Maybe that's why you picked up this workbook in addition to reading *Winning the War for Your Mind*. You are sick and tired of being pulled down by your enemy's lies. You are exhausted from being held back from an abundant life. You refuse to live that way anymore. You don't want to look in a mirror in ten years and see the same person with the same problems staring back at you.

You know your thoughts will control you, so it's time to start controlling your thoughts. The battle for your life is always won or lost in your mind. In the trenches, where you dig in with truth to get out of the ruts carved by lies. And you can't do it alone—because you can't.

Ultimately, you'll want to be totally dependent on God.

Maybe that's where you find yourself today. You know your life is always moving in the direction of your strongest thoughts, and you realize your thoughts have been taking you in the wrong direction for far too long. You feel overwhelmed and weighed down by reoccurring destructive thoughts. It's time for a change. You know it. You are ready for it. You have started the process, but now you feel a little shaky. You wonder what exactly is going to change.

It's okay if you don't feel like you can change. It's not up to you. You depend on God to help renew your mind.

How? When you practice God's presence—always mindful that he is near—then you will pray, and when you pray, it leads you to praise. Praising God is all about perspective. A change of perspective leads you to praise God, and praising God changes your perspective. It's time to stop focusing on what's wrong and look at what's right. Maybe take time each day to write down all the good things. Literally count your blessings and thank God for them.

You also need to commit to fighting the enemy of your soul and using the tools and weapons of faith God has given you. The devil's target is your mind. His weapon is his lies. He will never stop trying to deceive you. There are lies he's been telling you your entire life. Right now, he's seeking out opportunities to tell you new lies. He is probably taking a swing at you as you read this, and he will again in the next few minutes, hours, days, and weeks.

So, what do you do? In a fight, you're smart to keep both hands up to protect yourself. Think of prayer as one hand and praise as the other. To overcome the enemy and win the war for your mind, you need to *keep* both hands raised.

When someone raises both hands, it can also be to surrender or to celebrate a victory. When *you* raise both hands, to God, it is *both*. You surrender to God *and* you anticipate the victory that is already yours. Because you know you are more than a conqueror though him who loves you.

And that's how you win the war for your mind!

EXPLORING GOD'S WORD

One of the best ways to shift your focus from your old lies and negative thoughts to God's presence as the focus of your praise is to read through the Psalms. The psalmist often begins by acknowledging his worries, fears, and concerns—things like facing murderous enemies, feeling distant from God, being falsely accused, and experiencing painful disappointment.

From there, he then forces himself to praise God and reminds himself of what's true. For example, just consider, "Why, my soul, are you downcast? Why so disturbed within me? Put your hope in God, for I will yet praise him, my Savior and my God" (Psalm 42:5). Some psalms even take it a step further and seem to utilize a sandwich method. The speaker begins by praising God or proclaiming one of his attributes before bringing up whatever is bothering the psalmist. But then he closes his psalm by reassuring himself of what's true about God.

You can see this in the following psalm as David, identified as the psalmist here, envelops his negative thoughts in between assertions of spiritual truth:

> ¹ *The Lord is my light and my salvation—*
> *whom shall I fear?*
> *The Lord is the stronghold of my life—*
> *of whom shall I be afraid?*
>
> ² *When the wicked advance against me*
> *to devour me,*
> *it is my enemies and my foes*
> *who will stumble and fall.*
> ³ *Though an army besiege me,*
> *my heart will not fear;*
> *though war break out against me,*
> *even then I will be confident.*
>
> ⁴ *One thing I ask from the Lord,*
> *this only do I seek:*
> *that I may dwell in the house of the Lord*
> *all the days of my life,*
> *to gaze on the beauty of the Lord*
> *and to seek him in his temple.*
> ⁵ *For in the day of trouble*
> *he will keep me safe in his dwelling;*
> *he will hide me in the shelter of his sacred tent*
> *and set me high upon a rock.*

[6] Then my head will be exalted
  above the enemies who surround me;
at his sacred tent I will sacrifice with shouts of joy;
  I will sing and make music to the LORD.

[7] Hear my voice when I call, LORD;
  be merciful to me and answer me.
[8] My heart says of you, "Seek his face!"
  Your face, LORD, I will seek.
[9] Do not hide your face from me,
  do not turn your servant away in anger;
  you have been my helper.
Do not reject me or forsake me,
  God my Savior.
[10] Though my father and mother forsake me,
  the LORD will receive me.
[11] Teach me your way, LORD;
  lead me in a straight path
  because of my oppressors.
[12] Do not turn me over to the desire of my foes,
  for false witnesses rise up against me,
  spouting malicious accusations.

[13] I remain confident of this:
  I will see the goodness of the LORD
  in the land of the living.
[14] Wait for the LORD;
  be strong and take heart
  and wait for the LORD.

— PSALM 27:1–14

- Why do you think the psalmist asks rhetorical questions ("whom shall I fear? of whom shall I be afraid?") at the beginning of his prayer? Why not just say "I'm not afraid of anyone"?

- What is the "one thing" the psalmist asks of the Lord here? What danger is the speaker anticipating?

- After such a bold proclamation of faith in verses 1–6, what shift occurs beginning with verse 7? Why do you suppose the psalmist is suddenly thinking about the worst-case scenario of God abandoning him?

- Reread verses 7–12 and make a list of all the fears and concerns mentioned or implied by the psalmist. How does he invite God's presence into each of them?

- What's the source of the psalmist's confidence as he nears the end of the psalm in verse 13? Why does he remind himself of God's goodness "in the land of the living"?

- Considering all that's been covered in this psalm, why do you suppose the writer ends by emphasizing patience? What's the significance of waiting on God in light of everything mentioned here?

REFLECTING ON THE TRUTH

The psalmist knew that the secret of dealing with unwanted thoughts is to look through them and not at them. When you focus on your problems, you only see overwhelming obstacles and impossible barriers. When you look through your problems and see God's power, presence, and purpose, then your perspective changes. Just like David writes at the end of Psalm 27, you can be patient as you wait on God's timing and place your confidence in him.

- What words, phrases, or images jumped out at you as you read Psalm 27? Go back and underline or circle the ones that resonate with you most.

- What emotions does this psalm evoke in you? In which verses do you most identify with what David is saying?

- What does this psalm have in common with the way you typically pray to God? How do your prayers reveal both confidence and uncertainty, both fear and security?

- What attributes of God does David include in this psalm? Which of these attributes are you especially grateful to experience in your life right now?

- How does the psalmist pre-frame his vision of facing future enemies? How can you do the same with whatever you're facing right now?

- In what areas of your life are you currently waiting on God to move, guide, or direct you? What does it look like for you to "be strong and take heart" as the psalmist encourages you to do?

CHANGING YOUR STRATEGY

As you reach the end of this workbook experience, it's a good time to pause and assess all you've learned and what has changed in your thinking. Looking back through the previous lessons, try to think about your two most important takeaways from each. If you've made notes in the margins or underlined points in *Winning the War for Your Mind*, you will want to review them as well.

Take a few minutes to consider how your strategy for winning your mental and spiritual battles has changed in the last few weeks. Invite God into your assessment and ask for his ongoing help to win the war for your mind. Use the following questions to help you evaluate your experience during this study and move forward into sustained victory.

- Looking back through past lessons, what stands out to you now? Are there consistent themes or threads you see running throughout your experiences in the twelve lessons?

- How has your relationship with God changed over the course of completing this study? Where do you see evidence of this change in your notes, answers, and written reflections? In the way you make decisions and choose to act each day?

- How has the war for control of your thoughts changed since you started this workbook? What have you learned about defeating the enemy that wasn't clear to you before? What have you learned about God and how you relate to him?

- What passages or verses from the Bible have empowered you the most as you defeat the enemy and overcome his assaults? How do these truths help you see through the devil's lies?

- Make a list of at least five things that you're especially grateful for learning or experiencing while completing this workbook. Thank God for how he will continue to use them in your life.

• How will you continue your momentum now that you've completed this workbook and finished reading *Winning the War for Your Mind*? What's your action plan moving forward?

EXERCISING THE EXCHANGE

If you're not sure how to answer the last question in the previous section, don't panic. It's not easy to take what you've learned and put it into practice. But you don't want to lose your momentum and slide back into old neural ruts and negative thought patterns. You have made huge strides since you started this workbook. Simply choose to be deliberate about what and how you will incorporate all you've learned into your daily habits and routines.

Read through the Conclusion, "Choosing to Win the War," in *Winning the War in Your Mind*. Use a highlighter or underline the summary points, overall strategies, and specific tactics you need most. Write a new declaration, a kind of master battle plan moving forward, that you can read every day as a reminder of the victory in your mind and the changes in your behavior. (As part of this process, you may also find the afterword and appendix in the book to be helpful.)

Remember, you are moving in the direction of your strongest thoughts. But now you've learned to expose false beliefs, dangerous assumptions, and the lies of the enemy. Now you're focused on God's truth and his presence in your life. Now you praise God for all he's doing as you dwell on the blessings and collateral goodness all around you. When you struggle, you will remember that your experience plus God's presence is enough.

Your war may not feel like it's over, but rest in the confidence that your victory belongs to the Lord!

LEADER'S GUIDE

This workbook is a companion to *Winning the War in Your Mind*, and it's designed for both individuals and groups. If you're participating in a group study that has designated you as its leader, thank you for agreeing to serve in this capacity. What you have chosen to do is valuable and will make a great difference in the lives of others.

Winning the War in Your Mind is a twelve-session study built around individual completion of this workbook and small-group interaction. As the group leader, just think of yourself as the host of a dinner party. Your job is to take care of your guests by managing all the behind-the-scenes details so that when everyone arrives, they can just enjoy time together.

As group leader, your role is not to answer all the questions or re-teach the content—the book, this workbook, and the Holy Spirit will do most of that work. Your job is to guide the experience and create an environment where people can process, question, and reflect—not receive more instruction.

Make sure everyone in the group gets a copy of the workbook. This will keep everyone on the same page and help the process run more smoothly. If some group members are unable to purchase the workbook, arrange it so that people can share the resource with other group members. Giving everyone access to all the material will position this study to be as rewarding an experience as possible. Everyone should feel free to write in their workbooks and bring them to group every week.

SETTING UP THE GROUP

As the group leader, you'll want to create an environment that encourages sharing and learning. A church sanctuary or formal classroom may not be as ideal as a living room, because those locations can feel formal and less intimate. No matter what setting you choose, provide enough comfortable seating for everyone, and, if possible, arrange the seats in a semicircle so everyone can see the video easily. This will make group interaction and conversation more efficient and natural.

Also, try to get to the meeting site early so you can greet participants as they arrive. Simple refreshments create a welcoming atmosphere and can be a wonderful addition to a group study evening. Try to take food and pet allergies into account to make your guests as comfortable as possible. You may also want to consider offering childcare to those with children who want to attend. Managing these details up front will make the rest of your group experience flow smoothly and provide a welcoming space in which to engage the content of *Winning the War in Your Mind*.

STARTING YOUR GROUP TIME

Once everyone has arrived, it's time to begin the group. Here are some simple tips to make your group time healthy, enjoyable, and effective.

First, consider beginning the meeting with a short prayer, and remind the group members to put their phones on silent. This is a way to make sure you can all be present with one another and with God. Then, give each person one or two minutes to check in before diving into the material. In Session One, participants can introduce themselves and share what they hope to experience in this group study. Beginning with Session Two, people may need more time to share their insights from their personal studies and to enjoy getting better acquainted.

As you begin going through the material, invite members to share their experiences and discuss their responses with the group. Usually, you won't answer the discussion questions yourself, but you may need to go first a couple of times and set an example, answering briefly and with a reasonable amount of transparency. You may also want to help participants debrief and process what they're learning as they complete each session individually ahead of each group meeting. Debriefing something like this is a bit different from responding to questions about the material because the content comes from their real lives. The basic experiences that you want the group to reflect on are:

- *What was the best part about this week's individual study?*
- *What was the hardest part?*

- *What did I learn about myself?*
- *What did I learn about God?*

LEADING THE DISCUSSION TIME

Encourage all the group members to participate in the discussion, but make sure they know they don't have to do so. As the discussion progresses, you may want to follow up with comments such as, "Tell me more about that," or, "Why did you answer that way?" This will allow the group participants to deepen their reflections and invite meaningful sharing in a nonthreatening way.

While each session in this workbook includes multiple sections, you do not have to go through each section and cover every question or exercise. Feel free to go with the dynamic in the group and skip around if needed to cover all the material more naturally. You can pick and choose questions based on either the needs of your group or how the conversation is flowing. Also, don't be afraid of silence. Offering a question and allowing up to thirty seconds of silence is okay. It allows people space to think about how they want to respond and also gives them time to do so.

As group leader, you are the boundary keeper for your group. Do not let anyone (yourself included) dominate the group time. Keep an eye out for group members who might be tempted to "attack" folks they disagree with or try to "fix" those having struggles. These kinds of behaviors can derail a group's momentum, so they need to be steered in a different direction. Model active listening and encourage everyone in your group to do the same. This will make your group time a safe space and create a positive community.

At the end of each group session, encourage the participants to take just a few minutes to review what they've learned and write down one or two key takeaways. This will help them cement the big ideas in their minds as you close the session. Close your time together with prayer as a group.

Remember to have fun. Spending time with others and growing closer to God is a gift to enjoy and embrace. And get ready for God to change your thinking and change your life.

Thank you again for taking the time to lead your group. You are making a difference in the lives of others and having an impact on the kingdom of God.

ALSO AVAILABLE

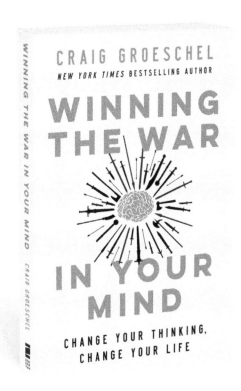

Are your thoughts out of control—just like your life? Do you long to break free from the spiral of destructive thinking? Let God's truth become your battle plan to win the war in your mind!

In this powerful new book, pastor and New York Times bestselling author Craig Groeschel provides you the tools that will change your mind and your life for the long-term.

Drawing upon Scripture and the latest findings of brain science, Groeschel reveals how to free yourself from the grip of harmful, destructive thinking and how to live the life of joy and peace that God intends you to live. *Winning the War in Your Mind* will help you:

- Learn how your brain works and see how to rewire it
- Identify the lies your enemy wants you to believe
- Recognize and short-circuit your mental triggers for destructive thinking
- See how prayer and praise will transform your mind
- Develop practices that allow God's thoughts to become your thoughts

God has something better for your life than your old ways of thinking. It's time to change your mind so God can change your life.

Available in stores and online!　　■ ZONDERVAN®

Also available from Craig Groeschel

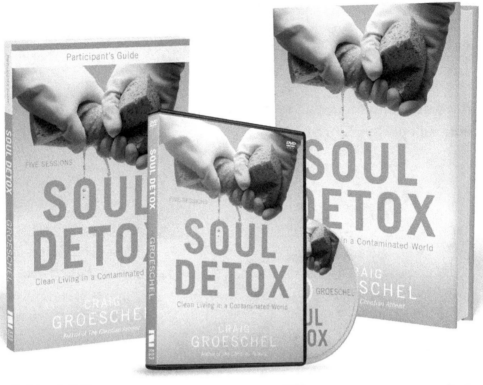

Participant's Guide	DVD	Book
9780310685760	9780310894919	9780310333821

In this five-session small group Bible study and book, pastor and best-selling author Craig Groeschel sheds light on relationships, thoughts, and behaviors that quietly compromise our well-being. Using concise teaching and honest humor, Groeschel provides a source of inspiration and encouragements for a faith-filled lifestyle that will keep you free of spiritual toxins.

Available now at your favorite bookstore,
or streaming video on StudyGateway.com.

Also available from Craig Groeschel

Book	Participant's Guide	DVD
9780310332220	9780310329756	9780310329794

You believe in God, attend church when it's convenient, and you generally treat people with kindness. But, have you surrendered to God completely, living every day depending upon the Holy Spirit?

In this six-session small group Bible study and book, pastor and author Craig Groeschel leads you and your group on a personal journey toward an authentic, God-honoring life. This honest, hard-hitting, and eye-opening look into the ways people believe in God but live as if he doesn't exist is a classic in the making.

Available now at your favorite bookstore,
or streaming video on StudyGateway.com.

ZONDERVAN®

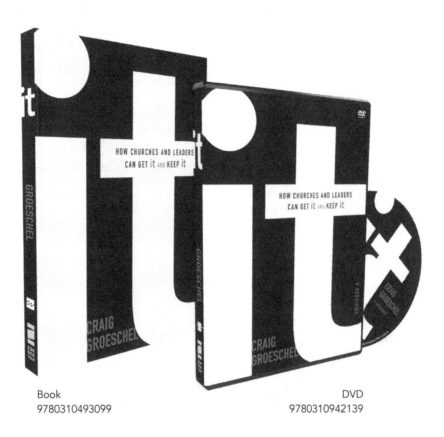

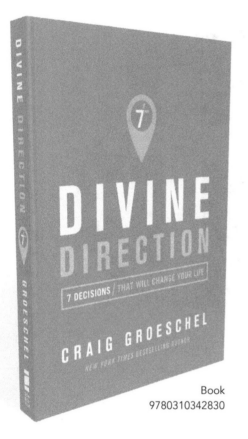

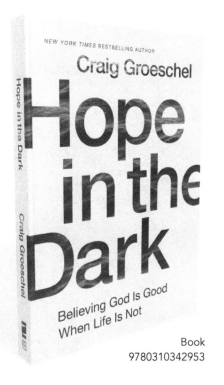

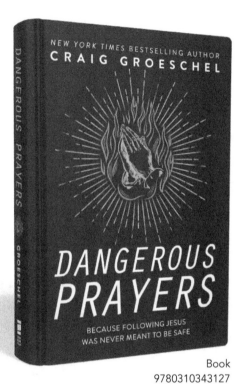

Printed in the USA
CPSIA information can be obtained
at www.ICGtesting.com
LVHW081200030624
781378LV00002B/2